pasta&pizza prego!

pasta&pizza prego!

DELICIOUS AND AUTHENTIC ITALIAN RECIPES

Gabriella Rossi

LORENZ BOOKS

First published in 1999 by Lorenz Books

© Anness Publishing Limited 1999

Lorenz Books is an imprint of
Anness Publishing Limited
Hermes House
88–89 Blackfriars Road
London SE1 8HA

This edition distributed in Canada by
Raincoast Books
8680 Cambie Street
Vancouver
British Columbia V6P 6M9

ISBN 0 7548 0081 4

A CIP catalogue record for this book is available from the British Library

Publisher: Joanna Lorenz
Project Editor: Linda Fraser
Designers: Patrick McLeavey & Jo Brewer
Jacket artwork and design: Clare Baggaley
Photographers: Karl Adamson, Steve Baxter, Edward Allright,
Amanda Heywood, David Armstrong & James Duncan
Recipes: Carla Capalbo, Shirley Gill, Sarah Gates,
Steven Wheeler, Elizabeth Martin, Catherine Atkinson, Annie Nichols,
Maxine Clark & Norma MacMillan
Illustrator: Anna Koska
Editorial Reader: Felicity Forster
Production Controller: Ben Worley

For all recipes, quantities are given in both metric and imperial measures,
and, where appropriate, measures are also given in standard cups and
spoons. It is important to follow one set, not a mixture, because they are
not interchangeable.

Previously published as two separate volumes, *The Little Pasta Cookbook* and
The Little Pizza Cookbook

Printed and bound in Singapore

3 5 7 9 10 8 6 4 2

Contents

Introduction

The recipes in this book are divided into two sections, Perfect Pasta and Delicious Pizzas. Ranging from the sublimely simple to the wickedly extravagant, all the recipes are easy to follow and are illustrated with an inspiring photograph of the finished dish. The introduction to each section offers down-to-earth advice on ingredients and techniques to help you make the most of these much-loved Italian foods. Whether you are cooking a quick supper for two or an authentic Italian dinner party for many, you will find the perfect menu within these pages.

Perfect Pasta

Singing the praises of pasta is rather like preaching to the converted; its popularity is phenomenal. Everyone loves pasta, from the toddler tucking into spaghetti hoops to the busy executive looking for a meal that won't take too long to prepare. Hungry teenagers and cash-strapped students eat huge piles of pasta; families find it the perfect food for mid-week meals; friends and lovers make a ritual of cooking and eating it together.

Pasta is convenient, easy to cook and very inexpensive. Composed largely of carbohydrate, it provides energy with very little fat. Marathon runners invariably dine on pasta before a big race. Slimmers find it filling, and it can form a very useful part of a calorie-controlled diet, so long as any sauces are sensibly selected. Nor do you have to forego the pleasure of eating pasta if you are unable to tolerate wheat. Pasta made from rice is now available, as are all sorts of pastas made from other grains, including barley, corn and buckwheat.

Dried pasta is the perfect store-cupboard ingredient. It has a long shelf life and can swiftly be turned into a meal with a simple sauce based on canned tomatoes or tuna. Fresh pasta is now widely available, and as it freezes well, it is equally convenient.

Pasta comes in an astonishing array of shapes, some of which are described in the following pages. From tiny stars for adding to soup to large shells for stuffing, there is a pasta shape for every occasion. Serve long thin pasta with a good coating sauce, while twists, quills or shells can take something more chunky. Flat noodles like tagliatelle make the perfect vehicle for a rich creamy sauce.

Some pastas now have subtle flavourings. Spinach and tomato types have been around for some time, but the range has now been extended to include mushroom, asparagus, smoked salmon, chilli, herb and the dramatic black pasta, which owes its colour to squid ink.

It would be easy to overlook oriental pastas, however there are so many of these that they could easily fill a book of their own. For a taster, try Chinese egg noodles or cellophane noodles, Japanese udon, or Thai rice flour noodles.

Oriental noodles tend to cook rapidly and are easily overcooked, so it is vital to follow the instructions on the packet.

Whether you serve pasta with a simple butter or oil dressing, toss it with a sauce, use it in a savoury bake or even a dessert, it is infinitely versatile. This collection of recipes proves the point, ranging as it does from tempting starters like Pasta with Prawns & Feta Cheese to dishes for easy entertaining such as Tagliatelle with Pea Sauce, Asparagus & Broad Beans. Along the way, you'll meet some old favourites, such as Fettuccine all'Alfredo, creamy Spaghetti alla Carbonara, and Macaroni Cheese. There are plenty of suggestions for vegetarians, and a tempting selection of simple pasta salads.

Familiar Pasta Types

CANNELLONI

These large hollow pipes are usually stuffed, topped with a sauce and grated cheese, then baked. Stuffed par-boiled cannelloni can also be deep fried.

MACARONI (MACCHERONI)

Athough this pasta was originally sold as long narrow tubes, somewhat thicker than spaghetti, the type most popular today is the little curved quick-cooking short-cut or elbow macaroni.

CONCHIGLIE

These shells come in various sizes, the largest being suitable for stuffing. Small ones are good for seafood salads.

FETTUCCINE

Often shaped into nests before packing, these flat ribbon noodles are particularly good with cream sauces.

FUSILLI

These twists or spirals come in various lengths. The short shapes are good with chunky sauces.

LASAGNE

Rectangular sheets of pasta, these are layered with sauces for one of the most popular baked pasta dishes.

CAPPELLINI/CAPPELLI DI ANGELO

Long, very thin pasta that is sometimes dried in coils to keep it from breaking. It takes its name from the Italian word for hair, and the coiled form is also known as angel hair pasta.

MAFALDE

Ruffled edges give these flat noodles an interesting appearance when cooked.

RUOTI

Children often like this wheel-shaped pasta.

SPAGHETTI

The name comes from the Italian word for string, a perfect description for the thin pasta strands. Spaghetti comes in a variety of flavours and colours: plain white, pinky-red tomato, green spinach and brown wholemeal. You may also find the white, red and green varieties in mixed packets.

TAGLIATELLE

These flat ribbon noodles made from egg pasta are usually dried in coils to prevent them breaking. A mixture of white and green tagliatelle is sometimes labelled as "paglia e fieno" (straw and hay). Like fettuccine, it's best served with a creamy sauce.

FARFALLE

The word means "butterflies" and the shapes are also referred to as bows, and they come in various sizes.

PENNE

Also known as quills, the term describes hollow pasta, cut on the slant into short lengths. Penne rigate is the ridged form.

11

TORTELLINI

These small stuffed pasta shapes need little by way of accompaniment, and are best served with either a very simple sauce, or, more usually, just olive oil or a little melted butter. The plainer varieties are sometimes added to soup.

Techniques

HOW MUCH PASTA DO YOU NEED?

Allow 50–75g/2–3oz per person for a starter; 115–175g/4–6oz for a main course which also includes a sauce. If you cook more pasta than you need, rinse the surplus under cold water, drain thoroughly and toss with a little oil. Place in a bowl, cover and leave to cool completely, then chill and use the next day as the basis for a salad, or to add to soup.

COOKING

Bring a large saucepan of salted water to a rapid boil. Add the pasta, stir well, then reduce the heat to keep the water at a rolling boil without allowing it to boil over. Stir the pasta once or twice more during cooking to keep the strands or shapes separate. Dried pasta will require about 8–12 minutes, but fresh pasta cooks far more rapidly and some strands or shapes will be ready as soon as they rise to the surface of the boiling liquid. Filled fresh pasta will take up to 5 minutes to cook.

TESTING

Using a slotted spoon, remove a strand or piece of pasta from the pan. Squeeze it between your fingers. It should break cleanly. The well-known Italian term is *al dente* (to the bite), which means that the pasta should be tender while retaining a degree of texture. As soon as the pasta is ready, drain it thoroughly. If you merely turn off the heat and leave it in the water, it will continue to cook and will rapidly become flabby.

SERVING

Have ready a warmed serving bowl. A large deep bowl is best as it will hold in the heat and give enough room for tossing. Place a knob of butter or a little olive oil in the bowl, add the drained pasta and toss well. If you are adding a creamy sauce omit the butter or oil. If the sauce is chunky, it is a good idea to toss the pasta with a small amount of sauce, then serve it with the remaining sauce piled on top.

12

TIPS

• Use wholemeal pasta for extra fibre, but cook in plenty of boiling water and check it frequently when cooking as it may absorb more liquid than plain pasta.

• Many cooks swear by adding a dash of oil to the water when cooking pasta. It is not absolutely necessary, but does help to keep the pieces or strands separate and also makes it less likely that the water will boil over.

• Look out for special large pasta pans with integral strainers: the pasta is cooked in an inner, perforated pan which sits inside the main pan. This not only makes draining extremely easy, it also prevents the pasta from sticking to the bottom of the pan during cooking.

• When cooking spaghetti, push the strands gently down into the pan so that they curl into the boiling water as they soften.

• Uncooked fresh pasta freezes well and can be cooked from frozen, although it will take marginally more time. Baked pasta dishes like lasagne also freeze well, but plain cooked pasta is not an ideal candidate, as it can be limp and soggy when thawed.

13

Starters &
Light Lunches

Pasta, Bean & Vegetable Soup

INGREDIENTS

*115g / 4oz / ¾ cup dried borlotti or black-eyed
beans, soaked overnight in water to cover
1.2 litres / 2 pints / 5 cups unsalted vegetable
or chicken stock
1 large onion, chopped
1 large garlic clove, finely chopped
2 celery sticks, chopped
½ red pepper, seeded and chopped
400g / 14oz can chopped tomatoes
225g / 8oz piece of smoked bacon loin
2 courgettes, halved lengthways and sliced
15ml / 1 tbsp tomato purée
75g / 3oz / ¾ cup tiny dried pasta shapes
for soup
salt and ground black pepper
shredded fresh basil, to garnish*

SERVES 4–6

1 Drain the beans and put them in a large heavy-based saucepan. Add fresh cold water to cover. Bring to the boil, boil hard for 10 minutes, then drain the beans in a colander. Rinse the beans under cold water, return them to the pan and add the stock. Bring to the boil, skimming off any foam that rises to the surface.

2 Add the onion, garlic, celery, red pepper, tomatoes and bacon (in the piece) to the pan.

3 Bring the liquid in the pan back to the boil, lower the heat, cover and simmer for 1½ hours or until the beans are just tender. Lift out the bacon, shred it coarsely with two forks and keep it hot.

4 Add the courgettes and tomato purée to the soup. Season if necessary, though it will probably be unnecessary to add salt. Simmer the soup for 5–8 minutes more, adding the pasta shapes towards the end of cooking so that they cook for no longer than the time suggested on the packet.

5 Stir in the shredded bacon. Serve the soup in heated bowls, with a sprinkling of shredded basil on top of each portion.

15

Pasta with Prawns & Feta Cheese

INGREDIENTS

450g/1lb/4 cups penne or other dried
pasta shapes
50g/2oz/¼ cup butter
450g/1lb medium raw prawns, peeled
and deveined
6 spring onions
225g/8oz feta cheese, cubed
small bunch fresh chives, snipped
salt and ground black pepper

SERVES 4

16

2 Meanwhile melt the butter in a second pan and add the raw prawns. Cook over a moderate heat for a few minutes until they turn pink. Slice the spring onions and stir in. Continue to cook gently for a further minute, stirring occasionally.

3 Add the feta cheese and half of the snipped chives to the prawn mixture. Toss it all lightly together to mix and then season with black pepper. When the pasta is just tender, drain it well, divide it among individual serving dishes and spoon the sauce on top. Serve sprinkled with the remaining chives.

1 Bring a large saucepan of lightly salted water to the boil. Add the pasta and cook for 10–12 minutes or according to the instructions on the packet.

VARIATION
Other slightly salty cheeses would also be good
— try Caerphilly, Cheshire or Gorgonzola.

Fresh Pea & Ham Soup

INGREDIENTS

115g/4oz/1 cup small dried pasta shapes
30ml/2 tbsp sunflower oil
6 spring onions, chopped
350g/12oz/3 cups frozen peas
1.2 litres/2 pints/5 cups chicken stock
225g/8oz raw unsmoked ham or gammon
60ml/4 tbsp double cream
salt and ground black pepper

SERVES 4

18

1 Bring a large saucepan of lightly salted water to the boil. Add the dried pasta shapes and cook for 10–12 minutes or according to the instructions on the packet, until it is *al dente*. Drain, refresh under cold water to avoid further cooking and drain again. Set the pasta aside until required.

2 Heat the oil in a large heavy-based saucepan. Cook the spring onions for several minutes until soft. Add the frozen peas and the chicken stock and bring to the boil. Lower the heat and simmer for 10 minutes until the mixture becomes very soft.

3 Purée the soup in a blender. Return it to the clean pan. Cut the ham or gammon into short fingers. Add these to the soup and simmer until cooked. Stir in the pasta and heat through gently for 2–3 minutes. Stir in the cream, season to taste, and serve in heated bowls.

Pasta Bows with Smoked Salmon & Dill

INGREDIENTS

450g / 1lb / 4 cups dried pasta bows (farfalle)
50g / 2oz / ¼ cup butter
6 spring onions, sliced
90ml / 6 tbsp dry white wine or vermouth
450ml / ¾ pint / scant 2 cups double cream
freshly grated nutmeg
225g / 8oz smoked salmon
30ml / 2 tbsp chopped fresh dill, plus
a few sprigs to garnish
½ lemon
salt and ground black pepper

SERVES 4

19

1 Bring a large saucepan of lightly salted water to the boil. Add the pasta and cook for 10–12 minutes or according to the instructions on the packet.

2 Heat the butter and fry the spring onions for about 1 minute. Add the wine and boil it away to 30ml/ 2 tbsp. Stir in the cream and add seasoning and nutmeg to taste. Bring to the boil, lower the heat and simmer for 2–3 minutes until slightly thickened.

3 Using a sharp knife, cut the smoked salmon into 2.5cm/1in pieces. Stir the pieces into the sauce along with the chopped dill. Squeeze in a little lemon juice to taste and check the seasoning. Keep the sauce warm until you are ready to serve it.

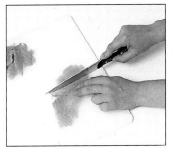

4 When the pasta is just tender, drain it well, toss it with the sauce and divide among heated serving dishes. Serve garnished with dill.

Fettuccine all'Alfredo

INGREDIENTS

450g/1lb dried fettuccine
25g/1oz/2 tbsp butter
210ml/7fl oz/scant 1 cup double cream
*50g/2oz/½ cup freshly grated Parmesan
cheese, plus extra to serve*
freshly grated nutmeg
salt and ground black pepper
dill sprigs, to garnish

SERVES 4

2 Meanwhile carefully melt the butter in 150ml/5fl oz/⅔ cup of the double cream in a large heavy-based saucepan. Bring the mixture to the boil, then lower the heat and simmer for about 1 minute until slightly thickened.

3 Drain the pasta well, add it to the cream sauce and toss it gently over the heat until all the strands are well coated in the sauce. Add the rest of the cream, with the Parmesan, nutmeg and salt and pepper to taste. Toss again until well coated and heated through. Serve at once, topping each portion with extra grated Parmesan and a sprig of dill.

1 Bring a large saucepan of lightly salted water to the boil. Add the pasta and cook for 10 minutes or for about 2 minutes less than the timing suggested on the packet. The pasta should still be a little firm to the bite (*al dente*) – don't let it overcook.

COOK'S TIP

Fresh fettuccine will cook much more quickly than dried pasta, and is ready as soon as it rises to the surface of the boiling water. When using fresh pasta, cook it at the last minute, after making the cream sauce. Fresh fettuccine is available from most good supermarkets.

20

Spaghetti Olio e Aglio

INGREDIENTS

450g/ 1lb dried spaghetti
120ml/ 4fl oz/ ½ cup olive oil
2 garlic cloves
30ml/ 2 tbsp chopped fresh parsley
salt and ground black pepper

SERVES 4

22

1 Bring a large saucepan of lightly salted water to the boil. Add the dried spaghetti and cook for 10–12 minutes, or according to the instructions on the packet, until it is *al dente*.

2 Meanwhile heat the olive oil in a saucepan. Using a sharp knife, peel and chop the garlic on a chopping board. Add it, with a pinch of salt, to the oil. Cook gently, stirring all the time, until the garlic has turned pale gold in colour.

3 As soon as the spaghetti is just tender, drain it well in a sieve and return it to the clean saucepan. Pour over the warm — but not sizzling — garlic and oil and toss gently until all the spaghetti strands are well coated. Add the chopped parsley along with plenty of ground black pepper and salt if required. Finally, thoroughly toss the spaghetti once more before serving.

Pasta Pronto with Parsley Pesto

INGREDIENTS

450g/1lb/4 cups dried pasta shapes
75g/3oz/¾ cup whole blanched almonds
50g/2oz/½ cup flaked almonds
40g/1½oz/¾ cup fresh parsley
2 garlic cloves, crushed
45ml/3 tbsp olive oil
45ml/3 tbsp lemon juice
5ml/1 tsp sugar
250ml/8fl oz/1 cup boiling water
salt
25g/1oz/¼ cup freshly grated Parmesan
cheese, to serve

SERVES 4

1 Bring a large saucepan of lightly salted water to the boil. Add the pasta and cook for about 10–12 minutes or according to the instructions on the packet, until it is *al dente*. Preheat the grill.

2 Keeping them separate, spread out the whole and flaked almonds in a grill pan. Toast them until golden. Set the flaked almonds aside.

3 Chop the parsley finely in a food processor or blender. Add the toasted whole almonds and process to a fine consistency. Add the garlic, olive oil, lemon juice, sugar and boiling water. Process the mixture until well combined.

4 When the pasta is just tender, drain it well and return it to the clean pan. Add half the sauce (the rest of the sauce will keep in a screw-topped jar in the fridge for up

to 10 days). Toss gently to coat. Serve at once in heated bowls, topping each portion with a little of the grated Parmesan cheese and a few of the toasted flaked almonds. Extra grated Parmesan cheese can be served separately, if liked.

Vegetarian
Dishes

Pasta with Spring Vegetables

INGREDIENTS

115g/4oz baby leeks, trimmed
225g/8oz asparagus spears, trimmed
1 small fennel bulb
115g/4oz broccoli florets, cut into tiny sprigs
115g/4oz/1 cup fresh or frozen peas
350g/12oz/3 cups penne or other dried
pasta shapes
40g/1½oz/3 tbsp butter
1 shallot, chopped
45ml/3 tbsp chopped fresh mixed herbs
300ml/½ pint/1¼ cups double cream
salt and ground black pepper
freshly grated Parmesan cheese, to serve

SERVES 4

1 Cut the leeks and asparagus diagonally into 5cm/2in lengths. Trim the fennel bulb and remove any tough outer leaves. Cut the fennel into wedges, leaving the layers attached at the root ends so that the pieces remain intact. Bring two large saucepans of lightly salted water to the boil.

2 Cook all the vegetables separately in one of the pans of water. As soon as each type is tender, transfer it with a slotted spoon to a bowl. Keep all of the vegetables hot. Add the pasta to the second pan of boiling water. Cook for 10–12 minutes or according to the instructions on the packet.

3 Melt the butter in a pan. Add the shallot and cook until softened but not browned. Stir in the herbs and cream. Cook for a few minutes, until slightly thickened.

4 Drain the pasta well, pile it into a heated bowl and add the sauce and cooked vegetables. Season and toss to mix. Serve with the Parmesan.

25

Spinach & Ricotta Conchiglie

INGREDIENTS

350g/12oz large dried conchiglie (shells)
450ml/¾ pint/scant 2 cups passata or
strained puréed canned tomatoes
275g/10oz frozen chopped spinach, thawed
50g/2oz fresh white breadcrumbs
120ml/4fl oz/½ cup milk
60ml/4 tbsp olive oil
225g/8oz/1 cup ricotta cheese
freshly grated nutmeg
1 garlic clove, crushed
2.5ml/½ tsp black olive paste (optional)
25g/1oz/¼ cup freshly grated Parmesan cheese
25g/1oz/⅓ cup pine nuts
salt and ground black pepper

SERVES 4

1 Preheat the oven to 180°C/350°F/Gas 4. Bring a large saucepan of lightly salted water to the boil. Add the pasta and cook for 10–12 minutes or according to the instructions on the packet. Refresh under cold water, drain and set aside.

2 Tip the passata into a nylon sieve set over a bowl. Press it against the sieve to remove excess liquid, then scrape the passata into a separate bowl. Discard the passata liquid, or save it for adding to soups or sauces. Wash the sieve, replace it over the clean bowl and repeat the process with the spinach.

3 Place the breadcrumbs, milk and 45ml/3 tbsp of the olive oil in a food processor or blender. Process to combine, then add the spinach and the ricotta cheese. Process briefly, then scrape the mixture into a bowl and add the nutmeg and salt and pepper to taste.

4 Add the garlic, remaining olive oil and olive paste (if using) to the passata. Spread the sauce evenly over the bottom of a flameproof dish. Spoon the spinach mixture into a piping bag fitted with a large plain nozzle and fill the pasta shapes (alternatively, fill with a spoon) and arrange them over the sauce in the dish. Cover the dish with foil and heat through in the oven for 15–20 minutes.

5 Preheat the grill. Remove the foil and scatter the Parmesan cheese and pine nuts over the filled conchiglie. Brown the topping under the grill and serve the dish at once.

26

Macaroni Cheese

INGREDIENTS

175g/6oz/1½ cups grated Parmesan cheese
or Cheddar, or a combination
40g/1½oz/¾ cup fresh white breadcrumbs
450g/1lb/4 cups short-cut macaroni or other
dried hollow pasta shapes
flat leaf parsley, to garnish
BÉCHAMEL SAUCE
475ml/16fl oz/2 cups milk
1 bay leaf
3 mace blades
50g/2oz/¼ cup butter
40g/1½oz/6 tbsp plain flour

SERVES 6

1 Make the béchamel sauce. In a small saucepan, heat the milk with the bay leaf and mace until just below boiling point. Set aside to infuse for about 30 minutes, then strain.

2 Melt the butter in a saucepan, stir in the flour and cook for 1 minute. Gradually add the flavoured milk, stirring constantly until the sauce boils and thickens. Remove the béchamel sauce from the heat, stir in three quarters of the cheese, then cover closely and set aside until required.

3 Preheat the oven to 200°C/400°F/ Gas 6. Grease a baking dish and sprinkle with half the breadcrumbs. Bring a large saucepan of lightly salted water to the boil. Add the pasta and cook for 7 minutes or according to the instructions on the packet.

4 When the pasta is just tender, drain it well and return it to the clean pan. Reheat the sauce, add it to the pasta and mix together until the pasta is completely coated. Spoon into the prepared dish, sprinkle with the rest of the grated cheese and remaining breadcrumbs and bake for 20 minutes. Garnish with flat leaf parsley and serve.

Pasta Napoletana

INGREDIENTS

450g / 1lb mafalde or other dried pasta
basil sprigs, to garnish
freshly grated Parmesan cheese, to serve
NAPOLETANA SAUCE
30ml / 2 tbsp olive oil
1 onion, finely chopped
1 carrot, finely diced
1 celery stick, finely diced
900g / 2lb ripe red tomatoes or 2 x 400g /
14oz cans chopped tomatoes
1 parsley sprig
pinch of caster sugar
120ml / 4fl oz / ½ cup dry white wine (optional)
15ml / 1 tbsp chopped fresh oregano
salt and ground black pepper

SERVES 4

1 Start by making the sauce. Heat the olive oil in a saucepan and add the onion, carrot and celery. Cook over a gentle heat for 5 minutes until the onion has softened but not coloured.

2 If using fresh tomatoes, chop them roughly with a sharp knife. Add the tomatoes (fresh or canned) to the pan, together with the parsley sprig, caster sugar and wine (if using). Bring to the boil, lower the heat and cook for 45 minutes until very thick, stirring occasionally.

3 Press the sauce through a sieve into a clean pan, or purée it in a food processor or blender and sieve it to remove the seeds. Add seasoning and oregano to taste and reheat the sauce gently.

4 Bring a large saucepan of lightly salted water to the boil. Add the pasta and cook for 10–12 minutes or according to the instructions on the packet. Drain well and toss with the sauce. Serve at once in heated bowls, topping each portion with the grated Parmesan cheese. Garnish with the basil.

Tortellini with Cream, Butter & Cheese

INGREDIENTS

*50g/2oz/¼ cup butter, plus extra
for greasing
300ml/½ pint/1¼ cups double cream
450g/1lb/4 cups fresh tortellini
115g/4oz Parmesan cheese in a piece
freshly grated nutmeg
salt and ground black pepper
fresh oregano, to garnish*

SERVES 4–6

30

1 Grease a flameproof serving dish generously with butter. Bring a large saucepan of lightly salted water to the boil. Melt the butter in a separate pan and stir in the cream. Bring to the boil and cook for 2–3 minutes, stirring until slightly thickened.

2 Cook the tortellini in the boiling water for 3–5 minutes, or according to the instructions on the packet, until it is *al dente*.

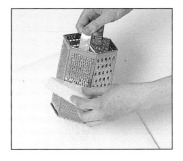

3 Grate all of the Parmesan cheese and add three quarters of it to the cream sauce. Stir the sauce frequently with a wooden spoon over a gentle heat, until the cheese has melted. Add the salt, pepper and nutmeg to taste. Preheat the grill to hot.

4 Drain the pasta and spoon it into the dish. Pour the sauce over the top and sprinkle with the rest of the cheese. Grill until golden and garnish with oregano.

Baked Tortellini with Three Cheeses

INGREDIENTS

25g / 1oz / 2 tbsp butter
450g / 1lb / 4 cups fresh tortellini
2 eggs
350g / 12oz / 1½ cups ricotta or curd cheese
25g / 1oz / ½ cup basil leaves, plus an extra sprig to garnish
115g / 4oz smoked cheese (such as smoked mozzarella or Cheddar), grated
60ml / 4 tbsp freshly grated Parmesan cheese
salt and ground black pepper

SERVES 4–6

1 Preheat the oven to 190°C/375°F/Gas 5. Grease a baking dish with the butter. Bring a large saucepan of lightly salted water to the boil. Add the tortellini and cook for 3–5 minutes or according to the instructions on the packet. Drain well.

2 Beat the eggs with the ricotta or curd cheese in a bowl. Add salt and pepper to taste. Spoon half of the tortellini into the prepared baking dish, then spread half of the the ricotta mixture over the top and cover with half of the basil leaves.

3 Sprinkle with the smoked cheese and the remaining basil leaves. Top with the rest of the tortellini and then spread the remaining ricotta mixture over the top.

4 Sprinkle evenly with the Parmesan cheese. Bake for 35–45 minutes or until golden brown and bubbling. Serve at once, garnished with basil.

Pasta Shells with Tomatoes & Rocket

INGREDIENTS

450g / 1lb / 4 cups pasta shells
45ml / 3 tbsp olive oil
450g / 1lb ripe cherry tomatoes, halved
75g / 3oz / 1½ cups fresh rocket leaves
salt and ground black pepper
freshly shaved Parmesan cheese, to serve

SERVES 4

2 Heat the oil in a large pan, add the cherry tomatoes and cook for about I minute. They should only just be heated through and must not disintegrate.

3 When the pasta is just tender, drain it well and add it to the tomatoes with the rocket. Toss gently to mix, taking care that the tomatoes do not break up.

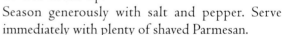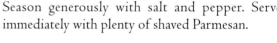

Season generously with salt and pepper. Serve immediately with plenty of shaved Parmesan.

I Bring a large saucepan of lightly salted water to the boil. Add the pasta and cook for 10–12 minutes or according to the instructions on the packet.

COOK'S TIP

Use a swivel vegetable peeler to shave the Parmesan. If you haven't got a vegetable peeler, you could use a very sharp knife instead to produce fine shavings.

Simple Suppers

Spaghetti alla Carbonara

INGREDIENTS

175g / 6oz rindless unsmoked streaky bacon
1 garlic clove, chopped
450g / 1lb dried spaghetti
3 eggs, lightly beaten
60ml / 4 tbsp freshly grated Parmesan cheese
salt and ground black pepper
small parsley sprigs, to garnish

SERVES 4

3 When the pasta is just tender, drain it quickly and add it to the saucepan containing the diced bacon and garlic. Stir in the lightly beaten eggs, a little salt, plenty of ground black pepper and half the Parmesan cheese. Toss well to mix (the heat from the pasta will cook the eggs to a creamy coating consistency). Serve in heated bowls with the remaining cheese either sprinkled on top or presented separately in a small bowl. Garnish with parsley.

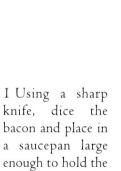

1 Using a sharp knife, dice the bacon and place in a saucepan large enough to hold the cooked spaghetti. Heat gently until the bacon fat runs, then add the garlic. Raise the heat to moderate and fry until the bacon is brown. Keep hot until required.

2 Bring a large saucepan of lightly salted water to the boil. Add the pasta and cook for 10–12 minutes or according to the instructions on the packet.

Penne with Aubergines & Mint Pesto

INGREDIENTS

*2 large aubergines, topped, tailed and cut
into short strips
450g/ 1lb/ 4 cups penne or other dried
pasta shapes
50g/ 2oz/ ½ cup walnut halves, chopped,
plus extra to garnish*
MINT PESTO
*25g/ 1oz/ ½ cup fresh mint
15g/ ½oz/ ¼ cup flat leaf parsley
40g/ 1½oz/ scant ½ cup finely grated fresh
Parmesan cheese
2 garlic cloves, roughly chopped
90ml/ 6 tbsp olive oil
salt and ground black pepper*

SERVES 4

1 Layer the aubergine strips in a colander, strewing each layer with salt. Leave to stand for 30 minutes over a plate to catch any juices. Rinse well in cold water, drain and pat dry on kitchen paper.

2 Make the mint pesto. Combine the mint, parsley, Parmesan and garlic in a food processor or blender. Process the mixture until smooth. With the motor running, add the oil in a steady stream until the mixture forms a thick mayonnaise-style sauce. Add salt and pepper to taste.

3 Bring a large saucepan of lightly salted water to the boil and add the dried pasta, then cook for about 8–10 minutes or according to the instructions on the packet, until *al dente*. About 3 minutes before the pasta is cooked, add the aubergine to the pan. Stir together to mix well and continue to boil in order to finish cooking the pasta.

4 Once the pasta is cooked, drain it along with the aubergine strips in a sieve or colander, then tip this mixture into a large bowl. Pour in half of the mint pesto and the chopped walnuts. Toss everything together well and serve immediately, topped with the remaining pesto and walnut halves.

COOK'S TIP
Aubergines are available from all good super-markets and greengrocers. They are either oblong or near-round in shape. Prime aubergines have a slight bloom to their shiny tough skin; the meaty flesh is yellow-green.

Pasta with Traditional Pesto

INGREDIENTS

1 garlic clove, crushed
25g/1oz/⅓ cup pine nuts
115g/4oz/½ cup curd cheese
25g/1oz/½ cup parsley sprigs
50g/2oz/1 cup fresh basil leaves
30ml/2 tbsp freshly grated Parmesan cheese
225g/8oz/2 cups fusilli (twists) or other dried pasta shapes
salt and ground black pepper
basil sprigs, to garnish

SERVES 4

1 First make the pesto. Put the garlic, pine nuts and curd cheese in a food processor or blender. Add half the parsley sprigs and half the basil leaves and process until smooth. Add the grated Parmesan cheese with the remaining parsley sprigs and basil leaves. Process until the herbs are finely chopped. Scrape the pesto into a bowl, add salt and pepper to taste and set aside until required.

2 Bring a large saucepan of lightly salted water to the boil. Add the fusilli or other pasta shapes and cook for 10–12 minutes or according to the instructions on the packet.

3 When the pasta is just tender, drain it very well, return it to the clean pan and add the pesto. Stir the pesto into the pasta taking care to ensure that all the pasta becomes fully coated. Serve in heated bowls, garnished with basil sprigs.

Tagliatelle with Sun-dried Tomatoes

Ingredients

1 garlic clove, crushed
1 celery stick, finely sliced
115g/4oz/1 cup sun-dried tomatoes,
finely chopped
90ml/6 tbsp red wine
8 plum tomatoes, peeled and roughly chopped,
or 400g/14oz can plum tomatoes, chopped
350g/12oz dried tagliatelle
salt and ground black pepper

SERVES 4

1 Mix together the garlic, celery, sun-dried tomatoes and wine in a saucepan. Cook over a gentle heat for 15 minutes, then stir in the chopped plum tomatoes and mix well. Add salt and pepper to taste, and leave the sauce to simmer while you cook the pasta.

2 Bring a large saucepan of lightly salted water to the boil, then add the pasta and cook for about 10–12 minutes or according to the instructions on the packet.

3 When the pasta is just tender, drain it well and return it to the clean pan. Toss the pasta with half the sauce. Serve in heated bowls, topped with the remaining sauce.

39

Baked Vegetable Lasagne

INGREDIENTS

30ml / 2 tbsp olive oil
1 onion, very finely chopped
500g / 1¼lb tomatoes, chopped
or 2 x 400g / 14oz cans chopped tomatoes
75g / 3oz / 6 tbsp butter
675g / 1½lb mushrooms, thinly sliced
2 garlic cloves, crushed
juice of ½ lemon
1 litre / 1¾ pints / 4 cups béchamel sauce
4-6 tbsp chopped fresh parsley
175g / 6oz / 1½ cups freshly grated Parmesan
cheese or Cheddar, or a combination
12 sheets no pre-cook lasagne
salt and ground black pepper

SERVES 6–8

1 Preheat the oven to 200°C/400°F/Gas 6. Heat the oil in a saucepan. Add the onion and cook for 10 minutes over a gentle heat until softened. Add the chopped tomatoes and cook for 6–8 minutes, stirring frequently. Season with salt and pepper to taste, turn down the heat to the lowest setting and simmer while you cook the mushrooms.

2 Melt half the butter in a frying pan and cook the mushrooms for a few minutes. Add the garlic, lemon juice, and seasoning to taste. Raise the heat and cook until the mushrooms start to brown. Meanwhile, stir the chopped parsley into the béchamel sauce.

3 Assemble the lasagne. Set aside 45ml/3tbsp of the grated cheese for the topping. Spread a fairly thin layer of the béchamel sauce in the bottom of a large shallow baking dish. Cover with a layer of lasagne. Add half of the mushroom mixture, then add a few spoonfuls of béchamel sauce and a sprinkling of cheese. Top with another layer of lasagne, then half of the tomato mixture, then béchamel and cheese as before. Repeat these layers until all the ingredients have been used, finishing with a layer of pasta coated with béchamel. Sprinkle with the reserved grated cheese and dot with the remaining butter. Bake for 30–40 minutes.

Pasta with Bolognese Sauce

INGREDIENTS

65g/2½oz/5 tbsp butter
75g/3oz pancetta or bacon in a piece, diced
1 onion, finely chopped
1 carrot, diced
1 celery stick, finely chopped
225g/8oz lean minced beef
115g/4oz/½ cup chicken livers, trimmed
and roughly chopped
30ml/2 tbsp tomato purée
120ml/4fl oz/½ cup white wine
200ml/7fl oz/scant 1 cup beef stock or water
freshly grated nutmeg
450g/1lb dried tagliatelle or spaghetti
salt and ground black pepper
freshly grated Parmesan cheese, to serve

SERVES 4–6

I Make the Bolognese sauce. Melt 50g/2oz/¼ cup of the butter in a small saucepan. Add the diced bacon and cook for 2–3 minutes until it starts to brown. Add the chopped onion, diced carrot and celery and cook, stirring frequently, until browned.

2 Stir in the beef and brown over a high heat. Stir in the livers and cook for 2–3 minutes, then add the tomato purée, wine and stock or water. Mix well. Season to taste with nutmeg, salt and pepper.

3 Bring the sauce to the boil, lower the heat and simmer for 35 minutes, stirring occasionally.

4 Bring a large pan of lightly salted water to the boil. Add the pasta and cook for 10–12 minutes or according to the instructions on the packet. Drain, return to the pan and toss with the remaining butter. Spoon on to plates and top each portion with some sauce. Serve with Parmesan cheese.

Pasta with Spinach & Anchovy Sauce

INGREDIENTS

*900g / 2lb fresh spinach or 500g / 1¼lb
frozen leaf spinach, thawed
450g / 1lb dried cappellini (angel hair pasta)
60ml / 4 tbsp olive oil
45ml / 3 tbsp pine nuts
2 garlic cloves, crushed
6 drained canned anchovy fillets, chopped
15g / ½oz / 1 tbsp butter*

SERVES 4

3 Heat the oil in a saucepan and fry the pine nuts until golden. Using a slotted spoon, transfer them to a bowl. Fry the garlic in the oil remaining in the pan until it turns pale golden. Add the drained anchovies and spinach to the pan and continue to cook for 2–3 minutes or until the sauce is heated through. Stir in the pine nuts.

4 When the pasta is just tender, drain it well, pile it into a heated dish and add the butter. Toss to coat. Pour the sauce over the top, fork it through roughly and divide among individual heated serving dishes.

1 If using fresh spinach remove any tough stalks, wash the leaves thoroughly and place them in a heavy-based pan with only the water that still clings to the leaves. Cover and cook over a high heat, shaking the pan occasionally, until the spinach is just wilted and is still bright green. Drain. If using frozen spinach, simply drain it thoroughly, pressing out excess moisture. Cut the spinach leaves into strips.

2 Bring a large saucepan of lightly salted water to the boil. Add the pasta and cook for 5–7 minutes or according to the instructions on the packet.

43

Pasta Salads

Tuna Pasta Salad

INGREDIENTS

*450g / 1lb ruoti (wheels) or other dried
pasta shapes
60ml / 4 tbsp olive oil
2 x 200g / 7oz cans tuna in oil, drained
and flaked
2 x 400g / 14oz cans cannellini or borlotti
beans, drained
1 small red onion, thinly sliced
2 celery sticks, thinly sliced
juice of 1 lemon
30ml / 2 tbsp chopped fresh parsley
salt and ground black pepper
flat leaf parsley, to garnish*

SERVES 6–8

3 Add the flaked tuna, beans, onion and celery to the bowl with the cold pasta. Lightly toss together all the ingredients using a wooden spoon, until well mixed.

4 Mix the lemon juice with the parsley. Add to the salad, with salt and pepper to taste, and toss lightly. Cover and leave to stand for at least 1 hour before serving, garnished with the flat leaf parsley.

45

1 Bring a large saucepan of lightly salted water to the boil. Add the pasta and cook for 10–12 minutes or according to the instructions on the packet.

2 When the pasta is just tender, drain it well, rinse it under cold water and drain again. Tip the pasta into a large bowl, add the olive oil and toss to coat. Set aside to cool completely.

Avocado, Tomato & Mozzarella Pasta Salad

INGREDIENTS

*175g/6oz/1½ cups farfalle (bows) or other
dried pasta shapes
6 ripe red tomatoes
225g/8oz mozzarella cheese
1 large ripe avocado
30ml/2 tbsp pine nuts, toasted
1 basil sprig, to garnish
DRESSING
30ml/2 tbsp wine vinegar
5ml/1 tsp balsamic vinegar (optional)
5ml/1 tsp wholegrain mustard
pinch of sugar
90ml/6 tbsp olive oil
30ml/2 tbsp shredded fresh basil
salt and ground black pepper*

SERVES 4

1 Bring a large saucepan of lightly salted water to the boil. Add the pasta and cook for about 10–12 minutes or according to the instructions on the packet. Drain well, rinse under cold water and drain again. Set aside to cool completely.

2 Using a sharp kitchen knife, slice the tomatoes and mozzarella into thin rounds. Cut the avocado in half, then remove the stone and peel off the skin. Slice the flesh lengthways. Arrange the tomatoes, mozzarella and avocado around the rim of a flat plate, overlapping the slices evenly.

3 Make the dressing. Mix the wine vinegar and the balsamic vinegar, if using, in a bowl with the wholegrain mustard and sugar. Add a little salt and pepper to taste, then gradually whisk in the olive oil using a small whisk or a fork.

4 Add the shredded basil and half the dressing to the pasta. Toss well to coat. Pile the pasta on to the plate in the centre of the avocado, tomato and mozzarella and drizzle with the remaining dressing. Scatter the pine nuts over the top and garnish with the basil sprig. Serve at once.

Tomatoes with Pasta Stuffing

INGREDIENTS

8 large firm tomatoes
115g/4oz/1 cup tiny dried pasta shapes for soup
8 black olives, stoned and finely chopped
45ml/3 tbsp finely chopped mixed fresh herbs
60ml/4 tbsp freshly grated Parmesan cheese
60ml/4 tbsp olive oil
salt and ground black pepper
flat leaf parsley, to garnish

SERVES 4

48

1 Preheat the oven to 190°C/375°F/ Gas 5. Slice the tops neatly off the tomatoes to serve as lids. Trim a thin slice off the bottom of any tomato which will not stand straight. Scoop out the tomato pulp into a sieve, taking care not to break the shells. Stand the shells upside down on kitchen paper to drain, placing the lids next to them.

2 Bring a large saucepan of lightly salted water to the boil. Add the pasta and cook for 2 minutes less than the time suggested on the packet. Drain well and tip into a bowl.

3 Add the olives, mixed herbs and Parmesan cheese to the bowl. Chop the drained tomato pulp and stir into the mixture with the olive oil. Season with plenty of salt and pepper.

4 Using a large spoon, stuff the tomatoes with the filling mixture and replace the lids. Arrange the completed tomatoes in a single layer in a well-oiled baking dish. Bake in the oven for 15–20 minutes. Remove and cool to room temperature before serving with or without the lids, garnished with flat leaf parsley.

Wholewheat Pasta Salad

INGREDIENTS

450g/1lb/4 cups wholewheat fusilli (twists)
or other dried pasta shapes
45ml/3 tbsp olive oil
2 small heads of broccoli, broken into tiny florets
175g/6oz/1½ cups frozen peas
2 carrots, finely chopped
1 red or yellow pepper, seeded and chopped
2 celery sticks, thinly sliced
4 spring onions, finely chopped
1 large tomato, diced
75g/3oz/½ cup stoned black olives
115g/4oz/1 cup diced Cheddar or
mozzarella cheese (optional)
flat leaf parsley, to garnish
DRESSING
45ml/3 tbsp wine or balsamic vinegar,
or a 2:1 mixture
15ml/1 tbsp Dijon mustard
15ml/1 tbsp sesame seeds
10ml/2 tsp chopped mixed fresh herbs,
such as parsley, thyme and basil
60ml/4 tbsp olive oil
salt and ground black pepper

SERVES 8

1 Bring a large saucepan of lightly salted water to the boil. Add the pasta and cook for 10–12 minutes or according to the instructions on the packet.

2 Drain the pasta well, rinse under cold water and drain again. Turn into a large bowl, toss with the olive oil and set aside to cool completely.

3 Boil the broccoli and peas until just tender. Refresh under cold water and drain well. Add to the cold pasta with the carrots, pepper, celery, spring onions, tomato and olives, and mix lightly.

4 Make the dressing by whisking the vinegar, mustard, sesame seeds and herbs in a bowl. Gradually whisk in the olive oil, then add salt and pepper to taste. Add the diced cheese to the salad, if using, then pour over the dressing and toss lightly. Cover and leave to stand for 15 minutes before serving, garnished with flat leaf parsley.

49

Pasta Salad with Olives

INGREDIENTS

450g/1lb/4 cups conchiglie (shells)
60ml/4 tbsp extra virgin olive oil
10 sun-dried tomatoes, thinly sliced
30ml/2 tbsp drained capers
115g/4oz/⅔ cup black olives, stoned
2 garlic cloves, finely chopped
45ml/3 tbsp balsamic vinegar
45ml/3 tbsp chopped fresh parsley
salt and ground black pepper

SERVES 4–6

50

1 Bring a large saucepan of lightly salted water to the boil. Add the pasta and cook for 10–12 minutes or according to the instructions on the packet. Drain well, rinse under cold water and drain again. Turn the pasta into a large mixing bowl and add the olive oil. Toss together until the pasta is well coated, then set the pasta aside to cool completely.

2 Place the sun-dried tomatoes in a bowl and pour a little hot water over them. Leave to soak for about 10 minutes, then drain, reserving the soaking liquid. Chop finely and put in a bowl. Add the capers, black olives, garlic and balsamic vinegar.

3 Add the tomato mixture to the pasta, with seasoning to taste. Toss well. Add 30–45ml/2–3 tbsp of the sun-dried tomato soaking water if the salad seems too dry. Toss with the parsley, cover and leave to stand for 15 minutes before serving.

Warm Pasta Salad with Ham, Egg & Asparagus

INGREDIENTS

450g/1lb asparagus spears, trimmed
1 small cooked potato, about 50g/2oz, diced
75ml/5 tbsp olive oil
15ml/1 tbsp lemon juice
10ml/2 tsp Dijon mustard
120ml/4fl oz/½ cup vegetable stock
450g/1lb dried tagliatelle
225g/8oz sliced cooked ham, 5mm/¼in
thick, cut into fingers
2 hard-boiled eggs, sliced
salt and ground black pepper
50g/2oz fresh Parmesan cheese, shaved

SERVES 4

1 Cut each asparagus spear in half and place the non-tip halves in a pan of boiling salted water for 12 minutes. Remove with a slotted spoon to a colander, refresh under cold water and drain.

2 Now add the asparagus tips to the pan of boiling water and cook for 6 minutes. Drain and refresh as for the thicker halves.

3 Roughly chop about 150g/5oz of the asparagus thicker halves, place in a food processor or blender and add the potato, oil, lemon juice, mustard and vegetable stock. Process to a smooth dressing. Pour into a jug and add salt and pepper to taste.

4 Bring a large saucepan of lightly salted water to the boil. Add the pasta and cook for 10–12 minutes or according to the instructions on the packet. Drain well,  rinse under cold water and drain again. Turn into a large bowl, add the asparagus dressing and toss to mix. Spoon on to individual plates, topping each portion with ham, hard-boiled eggs and the cooked asparagus tips. Serve with shavings of Parmesan.

Mediterranean Salad with Basil

INGREDIENTS

225g/8oz/2 cups penne rigate (ridged quills)
or other dried pasta shapes
175g/6oz fine green beans, trimmed
2 large ripe tomatoes, sliced or quartered
50g/2oz/1 cup basil leaves
200g/7oz can tuna in oil, drained and flaked
2 hard-boiled eggs, sliced or quartered
50g/2oz can anchovy fillets, drained
capers and black olives, to serve
DRESSING
30ml/2 tbsp white wine vinegar
2 garlic cloves, crushed
2.5ml/½ tsp Dijon mustard
30ml/2 tbsp shredded fresh basil
90ml/6 tbsp extra virgin olive oil
salt and ground black pepper

SERVES 4

1 Make the dressing. Whisk the vinegar, garlic, mustard and basil in a small bowl. Gradually whisk in the olive oil, then add salt and pepper to taste.

2 Bring a large saucepan of lightly salted water to the boil. Add the pasta and cook for 10–12 minutes or according to the instructions on the packet. Drain well, rinse under cold water and drain again. Turn into a bowl, add 30ml/2 tbsp of the dressing and toss to coat. Set aside to cool completely.

3 Bring a small saucepan of lightly salted water to the boil and add the trimmed green beans. Blanch for 3 minutes so they are crisp to the bite. Remove from the heat and drain, refresh under cold water to prevent further cooking and then drain again.

4 Arrange the tomatoes in the bottom of a shallow salad bowl. Moisten with a little of the remaining dressing and cover with a quarter of the basil leaves. Add the beans, in a neat layer, and moisten them with a little more dressing. Cover with a third of the remaining basil leaves.

5 Spoon the pasta into the bowl, cover with half the remaining basil leaves and arrange the tuna and the hard-boiled eggs on the top. Finally scatter all the anchovies, capers and black olives over the salad. Drizzle the remaining dressing over the top and garnish with the remaining basil leaves. Serve.

Dinner Party
Pasta

Fettuccine with Saffron Mussels

INGREDIENTS

1.75kg/ 4-4½lb fresh mussels, scrubbed
and bearded
2 shallots, chopped
150ml/ ¼ pint/ ⅔ cup dry white wine
generous pinch of saffron strands
350g/ 12oz dried fettuccine
25g/ 1oz/ 2 tbsp butter
2 garlic cloves, crushed
250ml/ 8fl oz/ 1 cup double cream
1 egg yolk
salt and ground black pepper
30ml/ 2 tbsp chopped fresh parsley, to garnish

SERVES 4

1 Place the mussels in a large saucepan. Add the shallots and wine. Cover tightly and cook over a high heat for 5–8 minutes, shaking the pan frequently, until the mussels have opened. Using a slotted spoon, remove the mussels from the pan. Discard any mussels that have not opened during the cooking process. Set aside a few of the mussels in their shells for garnishing; shell the rest and keep them hot until required.

2 Bring the cooking liquid remaining in the saucepan to the boil. Cook until it has reduced by half, then strain it into a jug, stir in the saffron strands and set aside.

3 Bring a large saucepan of lightly salted water to the boil. Add the pasta and cook for 10–12 minutes or according to the instructions on the packet.

4 Meanwhile melt the butter in a frying pan. Cook the garlic over a low heat for 1 minute, then pour in the saffron-flavoured mussel liquid and the cream. Heat gently until the sauce starts to thicken, then remove the pan from the heat and stir in the egg yolk and shelled mussels. Season to taste.

5 When tender, drain and season the pasta, then divide among serving plates. Spoon over the sauce and garnish with parsley and the reserved mussels.

Cannelloni al Forno

INGREDIENTS

15g/½oz/1 tbsp butter
*450g/1lb boned and skinned chicken
breasts, cooked*
225g/8oz mushrooms, trimmed and halved
2 garlic cloves, crushed
30ml/2 tbsp chopped fresh parsley
15ml/1 tbsp chopped fresh tarragon
1 egg, beaten
lemon juice (see method)
12-18 dried cannelloni tubes
600ml/1 pint/2½ cups Napoletana sauce
50g/2oz/½ cup freshly grated Parmesan cheese
salt and ground black pepper
flat leaf parsley sprigs, to garnish

SERVES 4–6

1 Preheat the oven to 200°C/400°F/Gas 6. Using the butter, generously grease a baking dish or shallow casserole large enough to hold all the cannelloni in a single layer. Chop the chicken roughly, then place it in a food processor fitted with a metal blade and chop it very finely. Scrape into a mixing bowl and set aside until required.

2 Add the mushrooms, garlic, parsley and tarragon to the food processor and process finely. Add to the chicken, then stir in the egg. Season with salt and pepper and add a dash or two of lemon juice.

3 Cook the cannelloni in boiling water if necessary (check the instructions on the packet) and drain well. Spoon the chicken mixture into a piping bag fitted with a large plain nozzle and fill the cannelloni tubes. Alternatively, fill the tubes with a spoon.

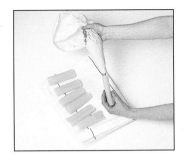

4 Put the tubes in the dish or casserole. Spoon over the sauce and sprinkle with the cheese. Bake for 30 minutes, until golden. Garnish with parsley.

COOK'S TIP

Mushrooms are sold either as buttons, cups or flats according to age. Use mushrooms on the day of purchase as they don't store well and go limp and lose their flavour quickly.

Tagliatelle with Gorgonzola Sauce

INGREDIENTS

450g / 1lb dried tagliatelle
5ml / 1 tsp cornflour
30ml / 2 tbsp dry vermouth
25g / 1oz / 2 tbsp butter, plus extra for
tossing the pasta
225g / 8oz Gorgonzola cheese
150ml / 5fl oz / ⅔ cup double or whipping cream
15ml / 1 tbsp chopped fresh sage
salt and ground black pepper

SERVES 4

1 Bring a large saucepan of lightly salted water to the boil. Add the pasta and cook for 10–12 minutes or according to the instructions on the packet.

2 Mix the cornflour with the vermouth in a cup. Melt the butter in a heavy-based saucepan. Crumble in 175g/6oz of the Gorgonzola and stir over a very gentle heat until the cheese melts. Pour in the cream, then whisk in the cornflour mixture. Stir in the sage, with salt and pepper to taste. Cook, whisking constantly, until the sauce thickens, then remove the pan from the heat.

3 When the pasta is tender, drain it, pile it into a large heated dish and toss in a knob of butter.

4 If it is necessary, reheat and whisk the sauce. Serve the pasta in heated bowls, topping each portion with sauce and the remaining cheese, crumbled on top.

58

Spaghetti with Seafood Sauce

INGREDIENTS

45ml / 3 tbsp olive oil
1 onion, chopped
1 garlic clove, crushed
225g / 8oz dried spaghetti
600ml / 1 pint / 2½ cups passata or strained,
puréed canned tomatoes
15ml / 1 tbsp tomato purée
5ml / 1 tsp dried oregano
1 bay leaf
5ml / 1 tsp sugar
115g / 4oz cooked prawns, peeled and deveined
175g / 6oz / 1½ cups cooked clam or cockle meat
(rinsed and drained if canned or bottled)
15ml / 1 tbsp lemon juice
45ml / 3 tbsp chopped fresh parsley
25g / 1oz / 2 tbsp butter
salt and ground black pepper
4 whole cooked prawns, to garnish (optional)

SERVES 4

1 Heat the oil in a saucepan. Add the onion and garlic. Cook over a moderate heat for 6–7 minutes, until the onion has softened.

2 Meanwhile bring a large saucepan of lightly salted water to the boil. Add the dried spaghetti and cook for 10–12 minutes, or according to the instructions on the packet, until it is *al dente*.

3 Stir the passata or strained tomatoes into the onion. Add the tomato purée, oregano, bay leaf and sugar. Bring to the boil, then lower the heat and simmer for 2–3 minutes. Stir in the shellfish, lemon juice and two thirds of the parsley. Cover and cook for 6–7 minutes. Season to taste.

4 When the spaghetti is just tender, drain it well and return it to the clean pan. Add the butter and toss until completely coated. Divide the spaghetti among four heated bowls and top with the seafood sauce. Garnish with the remaining parsley and the whole prawns, if using.

59

Prawns with Pasta & Pesto in Packets

INGREDIENTS

750g/ 1½lb whole medium raw prawns
450g/ 1lb tagliatelle or similar pasta
150ml/ 5fl oz/ ⅔ cup fresh pesto sauce or
ready-made equivalent
20ml/ 4 tsp olive oil
1 garlic clove, crushed
100ml/ 4fl oz/ ½ cup dry white wine
salt and ground black pepper

SERVES 4

1 Preheat the oven to 200°C/400°F/Gas 6. Twist the heads off the prawns and discard.

2 Cook the pasta in plenty of boiling salted water for 2 minutes, then drain. Mix with half the pesto.

3 Cut four 30cm/12in squares of greaseproof paper and put 5ml/1 tsp olive oil in the centre of each. Pile equal amounts of the pasta mixture in the middle of each square.

4 Top each square with prawns and spoon the remaining pesto, mixed with the garlic, over the top. Season with pepper and sprinkle the wine among them.

5 Brush the edges of the paper lightly with water and bring them loosely up around the filling, twisting them tightly to enclose the filling.

6 Place the parcels on a baking sheet and bake for 10–15 minutes. Serve them immediately, allowing each person to open his or her own pasta packet.

COOK'S TIP

Try using other fresh fish and seafood instead of prawns, if you prefer.

60

Linguine with Prosciutto & Parmesan

INGREDIENTS

115g/4oz prosciutto
450g/1lb dried linguine
75g/3oz/6 tbsp butter
50g/2oz/½ cup freshly grated Parmesan cheese
salt and ground black pepper
a few fresh sage leaves, to garnish

SERVES 4

1 Using a sharp knife, cut the prosciutto into strips the same width as the linguine. Bring a large saucepan of lightly salted water to the boil. Add the linguine and cook for 10–12 minutes, or according to the instructions on the packet, until it is *al dente*.

2 Meanwhile melt the butter gently in a second small saucepan. Stir in all the prosciutto strips and heat them through gently, taking care not to fry them.

3 When the linguine is ready, drain it well then divide it among four individual heated serving plates. Sprinkle the Parmesan cheese over the top, then pour over the buttery prosciutto strips and season with plenty of black pepper. (Since the cheese is salty, salt need not be added.) Serve at once, garnished with the sage leaves. You may also like to serve this dish with some additional grated Parmesan cheese in a separate, small serving bowl.

Spaghetti with Black Olive & Mushroom Sauce

INGREDIENTS

15ml / 1 tbsp olive oil
1 garlic clove, chopped
225g / 8oz mushrooms, chopped
150g / 5oz / 2/3 cups stoned black olives
30ml / 2 tbsp chopped fresh parsley
1 red chilli, seeded and chopped
450g / 1lb dried spaghetti
225g / 8oz cherry tomatoes
slivers of Parmesan cheese, to garnish

SERVES 4

1 Heat the oil in a large saucepan and cook the garlic over a gentle heat for 1 minute. Add the mushrooms, raise the heat a little and cover. Cook for 5 minutes.

2 Tip the mushroom mixture into a food processor or blender. Add the olives, parsley and chilli. Process until smooth, then scrape into a bowl and set aside. Bring a large saucepan of lightly salted water to the boil. Add the spaghetti and cook for 10–12 minutes, or according to the instructions on the packet, until it is *al dente*.

3 Meanwhile heat an ungreased frying pan, add the cherry tomatoes and shake the pan over a moderate heat for 2–3 minutes until the skins start to split.

4 Drain the pasta, return it to the clean pan and add the olive mixture. Toss to coat. Serve the pasta topped with the tomatoes and garnished with the Parmesan.

63

Tagliatelle with Pea Sauce, Asparagus & Broad Beans

INGREDIENTS

15ml/ 1 tbsp olive oil
1 garlic clove, crushed
6 spring onions, thinly sliced
225g/ 8oz/ 2 cups frozen peas, thawed
350g/ 12oz young asparagus spears
*30ml/ 2 tbsp chopped fresh sage, plus extra
leaves to garnish*
finely grated rind of 2 lemons
450ml/ ¾ pint/ scant 2 cups vegetable stock
225g/ 8oz frozen broad beans, thawed
450g/ 1lb dried tagliatelle
60ml/ 4 tbsp natural yogurt
salt and ground black pepper

SERVES 4

1 Heat the oil in a large pan. Add the garlic and spring onions and cook gently for about 2–3 minutes. Stir in the peas and one third of the asparagus, with all the chopped sage, lemon rind and stock or water. Simmer for 10 minutes, until the asparagus is tender. Purée in a food processor or blender until smooth, then return the sauce to the clean pan.

2 Pinch the broad beans between your fingers to pop off the skins, revealing the tender green beans. Discard the skins. Bring a small pan of water to the boil. Cut the remaining asparagus into 5cm/2in lengths, add it to the boiling water and cook until just tender. Drain well.

3 Bring a large pan of lightly salted water to the boil. Add the pasta and cook for 10–12 minutes or according to the instructions on the packet.

4 Add the cooked asparagus and the beans to the pea sauce. Stir in the yogurt and reheat gently – do not allow the sauce to boil. Season with salt and pepper.

5 When the pasta is just tender, drain it well and divide it among heated serving plates. Spoon the pea sauce over the pasta, garnish with some fresh sage, and serve at once.

64

Cannelloni

INGREDIENTS

8 dried cannelloni tubes
115g/4oz spinach leaves, trimmed
FILLING
15ml/1 tbsp sunflower oil
175g/6oz minced beef
2 garlic cloves, crushed
30ml/2 tbsp plain flour
120ml/4fl oz/½ cup beef stock
1 small carrot, finely chopped
1 small yellow courgette, chopped
salt and ground black pepper
SAUCE
25g/1oz/2 tbsp butter
15g/½oz/2 tbsp plain flour
250ml/8fl oz/1 cup milk
50g/2oz/½ cup freshly grated
Parmesan cheese

SERVES 4

1 Preheat the oven to 180°C/350°F/Gas 4. Make the filling. Heat the oil in a large saucepan, add the minced beef and break it up with a spoon. Stir in the garlic and cook for 5 minutes.

2 Stir in the flour and cook for 1 minute more. Add the stock, stirring all the time, and bring to the boil. Add the chopped carrot and courgette, with plenty of salt and pepper. Cook for 10 minutes.

3 Spoon the filling into the cannelloni tubes and arrange them in a single layer in a baking dish. Bring a small saucepan of water to the boil, blanch the spinach leaves for 3 minutes, then drain them well and arrange on top of the cannelloni.

4 Make the sauce. Melt the butter in a saucepan. Stir in the flour and cook for 1 minute. Gradually add the milk, stirring until the mixture boils and thickens. Add the cheese and stir over the heat until it melts.

5 Pour the sauce over the cannelloni and spinach. Bake for 30 minutes or until the topping is golden. Serve with tomatoes and a mixed leaf salad.

Delicious Pizzas

It can be no accident that the pizza has become one of the world's most popular foods. What could be more delicious than a crisp dough crust spread with a flavoursome tomato sauce, topped with your favourite ingredients and then covered in golden melted cheese? A meal in itself, served solo or with salad, pizza is enjoyed by people of all ages and is perfect for every occasion, from a child's birthday party to an after-theatre snack. Pizzettes are perfect for picnics, and calzonetti are even better, since the filling is neatly trapped inside the dough until you take that first bite.

With pizza dough so easy to make, why stake out the take-away? Just mix the ingredients, work out your frustrations on the dough and leave it to rise while

you make the topping of your choice. Prepare a large quantity of the basic tomato sauce in advance, so that there will be some ready when you need it, and have a few flavoured oils handy for adding extra interest.

Experienced pizza cooks don't roll out their dough — at least, not for more than a couple of strokes. They lovingly lift, tease and stretch it to fit their tins. Mastering the art is great fun, which the whole family can enjoy, even if they only stand on the sidelines and laugh at your efforts!

A pizza party is a very successful way to entertain. Supply plenty of dough, a large selection of toppings and four or five different types of grated cheese, including mozzarella and Parmesan.

Borrow extra baking sheets, and have the oven hot before the first guests arrive. Few will be able to resist the opportunity to make their own pizza, and the kitchen will fast become the focus of the party, with friendships forming and competition hotting up over who can produce the most interesting topping.

If you need inspiration, just leaf through this collection of recipes. Caramelized onion and salami, smoked chicken with yellow peppers, roast vegetables with goat's cheese, mussels with leeks – there is a combination for every occasion and a treat for every taste.

For a quick snack or supper, just add a topping to a French stick or ready-made base, or try a scone pizza. There is a recipe in this collection which does not even require an oven. You cook the pizza first in a pan and then finish it off under the grill.

An easy way to cope with unexpected visitors is to offer them a tray-baked Farmhouse Pizza. The wonderful combination of tomato sauce with mushrooms, smoked ham, artichokes and anchovies is always a favourite. Spread the topping equally over the entire pizza, or section it so that guests can avoid any ingredients they don't like.

Mini pizzas make great cocktail snacks if you add sophisticated toppings such as prawn and avocado or smoked salmon and crème fraîche. Deep-fried Spinach and Ricotta Panzerotti are equally popular. Thin and crispy or deep-pan indulgence, mouth-watering morsels or family feasts, pizzas never fail to rise to the occasion.

Tip-Top Toppings

ANCHOVIES

Canned anchovies make a marvellous pizza topping. They should be used straight from the drained can, but if you find them a little too salty, soak them in milk first.

ARTICHOKE HEARTS

These come canned in brine or bottled in oil. The latter are preferred for pizzas. Cut into thin slices, or chop as a filling for panzerotti.

BASIL

Known for its affinity with tomatoes, basil is a favourite pizza herb. Tear the leaves, rather than chopping them.

CAPERS

The preserved flower buds of a Mediterranean shrub, capers have a strong piquant flavour.

CHEESES

Mozzarella and Parmesan are obvious choices, but goat's cheese, Gorgonzola, Dolcelatte and mature Cheddar are also excellent. Smoked cheeses are a successful variation.

GARLIC

Garlic is added for accent, but is also wonderful as a pizza topping in its own right. Whole cloves of garlic can be roasted on top of the pizza for a marvellously mellow flavour.

MUSHROOMS

Button mushrooms are widely used (fry them first to make sure all the juices have evaporated). Try wild mushrooms too.

OLIVES

Fully ripe black olives are preferred for pizzas, providing a lovely colour contrast against the red of a rich tomato sauce.

ONIONS

Onions are usually fried before being used as a topping. Red onions look great on pizzas, especially with salami.

OREGANO

Often known as the "pizza herb", oregano can be worked into the dough or sprinkled over the topping just before baking.

PEPPERONI

An Italian cured sausage made from beef, pork and red peppers, pepperoni is available both whole and sliced in supermarkets.

PEPPERS

Strips of these brightly coloured vegetables add colour and flavour. Use peppers fresh or grill them for a special smoky taste.

PESTO

Natural basil pesto and red pesto (with added sun-dried tomatoes) are used for flavouring.

PINEAPPLE

Canned pineapple chunks are the children's favourite, especially with ham.

SWEETCORN

Drained canned sweetcorn kernels do not contribute a great deal of flavour, but add colour and texture.

TAPENADE

A paste which is made from green or black olives, ground with olive oil and seasoning, tapenade is tasty when spread on pizza bases, or spooned on top just before serving. It is especially good with goat's cheese.

71

TOMATOES

The absolute essential: use fresh plum or vine tomatoes, or canned chopped tomatoes. Always drain tomatoes well, though, or your pizza base will become soggy.

TOMATO PURÉE

Tomato purée is marvellous for adding extra flavour, especially to tomato sauce.

TUNA

Drained canned tuna makes a good topping and is often used on a Four Seasons pizza.

Techniques

BASIC PIZZA DOUGH
Makes one 30cm/12in base

Sift 175g/6oz/1½ cups strong white flour and 1.25ml/¼ tsp salt into a large mixing bowl. Stir in 5ml/1 tsp easy-blend dried yeast. Make a well in the centre and add 15ml/1 tbsp olive oil, with enough hand-hot water to make a soft, malleable dough. The amount will vary according to the absorbency of the flour, but you should not need more than 150ml/¼ pint/⅔ cup.

Turn the dough on to a lightly floured surface and knead for about 10 minutes, until smooth and elastic. Return it to the clean bowl. Cover with clear film and leave in a warm place for about an hour, until the dough has doubled in bulk.

Knock back the dough, turn it on to a lightly floured surface and knead again for 2–3

minutes. Roll out and use as directed, pushing up the dough edges to make a rim before adding the topping.

VARIATIONS
• *Deep-pan Pizza Dough*: Increase the amount of flour to 225g/8oz/2 cups and the salt to 2.5ml/½ tsp. Use 30ml/2 tbsp oil, but do not increase the amount of yeast.
• *Wholemeal Pizza Dough*: Use half wholemeal and half strong white flour. Add more water, if necessary.
• *Food Processor Dough*: Process the flour, salt and yeast briefly in a food processor. With the motor running, add the liquid through the feeder tube until the dough forms a soft ball. Rest for 2 minutes, then process for 1 minute to knead the dough. Put the dough in a bowl, cover and prove as for Basic Pizza Dough.

MAKING TOMATO SAUCE

Master the art of making a flavoursome tomato sauce, and not only will your pizzas taste superb, but you will have the ideal topping for pasta. Heat 15ml/1 tbsp olive oil in a saucepan and add 1 finely chopped onion with 1 crushed garlic clove. Fry over a gentle heat for 5 minutes, until softened, then add a 400g/14oz can of chopped tomatoes. Stir in 15ml/1 tbsp each of tomato purée and chopped fresh mixed herbs, with salt and pepper to taste. Add a pinch of sugar to bring out the flavour of the tomatoes.

Bring to the boil, then lower the heat and simmer, stirring occasionally, for 15–20 minutes, by which time the sauce will have reduced to a thick pulp. Leave to cool.

FLAVOURING OILS

Oil is brushed over the pizza base before the topping is added. Where appropriate, use the oil from a bottle of sun-dried tomatoes, or make your own flavoured oils.

Chilli Oil: Heat 150ml/¼ pint/⅔ cup olive oil in a saucepan until very hot, but not smoking. Carefully stir in 10ml/2 tsp tomato purée and 15ml/1 tbsp dried red chilli flakes. Leave to cool, then pour into a small jar. Cover and store in the fridge for up to 2 months (the longer you keep it the hotter it will become).

Garlic Oil: Put 4 peeled garlic cloves in a small jar. Pour in 120ml/4fl oz/½ cup olive oil. Cover the jar and store in the fridge for up to 1 month.

73

Classic Pizzas

Pizza Napoletana

INGREDIENTS

30cm/12in pizza base
30ml/2 tbsp olive oil
6 plum tomatoes
2 garlic cloves, chopped
115g/4oz/⅔ cup mozzarella cheese, grated
50g/2oz can anchovy fillets, drained and chopped
15ml/1 tbsp chopped fresh oregano
30ml/2 tbsp grated Parmesan cheese
ground black pepper

SERVES 2–4

3 Mix the mozzarella cheese and anchovies in a bowl. Sprinkle the mixture over the pizza, followed by the chopped fresh oregano and Parmesan. Drizzle over

the remaining oil and season with black pepper. Bake for 15–20 minutes or until the crust is crisp and golden. Serve at once.

1 Preheat the oven to 220°C/425°F/Gas 7. Brush the pizza base with 15ml/1 tbsp of the oil. Cut a small cross in the stalk end of each tomato. Place in a bowl and pour over boiling water to cover. Leave for about a minute, until the skins start to split, then drain and plunge into cold water. Gently slip off the skins.

2 Using a serrated knife, chop the tomatoes roughly. Spoon them over the pizza base to within 1cm/½ in of the rim, then sprinkle over the garlic.

Four Seasons Pizza

INGREDIENTS

450g / 1lb peeled plum tomatoes or 2
400g / 14oz cans chopped tomatoes, drained
45ml / 3 tbsp olive oil
115g / 4oz / 1 cup mushrooms, thinly sliced
1 garlic clove, crushed
30cm / 12in pizza base
350g / 12oz / 2 cups finely diced mozzarella
cheese
4 thin slices of cooked ham, cut into 5cm / 2in
squares
8 stoned black olives
2 drained bottled artichoke hearts in oil, halved
5ml / 1 tsp fresh oregano
salt and ground black pepper

SERVES 2–4

1 Preheat the oven to 220°C/425°F/ Gas 7. Strain the tomatoes through the medium holes of a food mill or sieve placed over a bowl, scraping in all the pulp. If you

use canned tomatoes, drain them for 10 minutes before straining, or the topping will be too sloppy.

2 Heat 30ml/2 tbsp of the oil in a frying pan. Cook the mushrooms over a moderately high heat for about 5 minutes, until they are golden and most of the juices have evaporated. Stir in the garlic and set aside.

3 Then spread the tomatoes over the pizza base to within 1cm/½in of the pizza rim. Sprinkle evenly with the diced mozzarella. Using a spatula, lightly

mark the pizza in quarters. Spread the mushrooms evenly over one quarter.

4 Arrange the ham squares in a second quarter and the olives and artichoke hearts on the remaining quarters. Sprinkle with oregano, salt and pepper, then drizzle the remaining olive oil over the top.

5 Bake for 15–20 minutes or until the crust is crisp and golden. Serve at once.

VARIATION
Add flaked drained tuna to the artichokes, if you like, and rounds of pepperoni to the mushrooms. The point with this pizza is that you can add whatever you like so long as the flavours do not clash.

Pizza Margherita

INGREDIENTS

30cm/12in pizza base
30ml/2 tbsp olive oil
1 quantity Tomato Sauce
150g/5oz mozzarella cheese
2 ripe tomatoes, thinly sliced
6–8 fresh basil leaves
30ml/2 tbsp grated Parmesan cheese
ground black pepper

SERVES 2–4

78

1 Preheat the oven to 220°C/425°F/ Gas 7. Brush the pizza base with 15ml/1 tbsp oil. Spread the tomato sauce over the base to within 1cm/ ½in of the rim.

2 Cut the mozzarella into thin slices. Then arrange the fresh tomato and mozzarella slices alternately in concentric circles on top of the pizza base.

3 Tear the basil leaves roughly and sprinkle them over the pizza, then sprinkle with the Parmesan. Drizzle over the remaining olive oil and season with black pepper. Bake for 15–20 minutes or until the crust is crisp and golden. Serve at once.

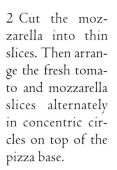

Four Cheeses Pizzas

INGREDIENTS

1 quantity Basic Pizza Dough
15ml / 1 tbsp Garlic Oil
½ small red onion, very thinly sliced
50g/2oz Dolcelatte cheese
50g/2oz mozzarella cheese
50g/2oz/½ cup grated Gruyère cheese
30ml/2 tbsp grated Parmesan cheese
15ml/1 tbsp chopped fresh thyme
ground black pepper

SERVES 4

1 Preheat the oven to 220°C/425°F/Gas 7. Grease two large baking sheets. Divide the dough into four pieces and roll each one out on a lightly floured surface to a 13cm/5in round. Place well apart on the greased baking sheets, then push up the edge of the dough on each round to make a thin rim.

2 Then brush each round with garlic oil and top with the red onion. Cut the Dolcelatte and mozzarella into cubes and scatter over the pizza bases. Mix the Gruyère, Parmesan and thyme in a bowl. Sprinkle the mixture over the pizzas.

3 Grind plenty of black pepper over the pizzas and bake in the oven for 15–20 minutes or until the crust on each pizza is crisp and golden. Serve at once.

Calzoni

INGREDIENTS

1 quantity Basic Pizza Dough
350g/12oz/1½ cups ricotta cheese
175g/6oz cooked ham, finely diced
6 tomatoes, peeled, seeded and diced
8 fresh basil leaves
175g/6oz/1 cup diced mozzarella cheese
60ml/4 tbsp grated Parmesan cheese
salt and ground black pepper
olive oil, for brushing

SERVES 4

1 Preheat the oven to 220°C/425°F/ Gas 7. Lightly grease two large baking sheets. Divide the dough into four pieces and roll each one out on a lightly floured surface to a 15cm/6in round.

2 Mix the ricotta, ham and diced tomatoes in a bowl. Tear the basil leaves roughly into pieces and add them to the bowl, with the mozzarella and Parmesan. Mix well and add plenty of salt and pepper.

3 Divide the filling equally between the four dough rounds, placing it on one half of each round and leaving a 2.5cm/1in border around the edge.

Dampen the edges with a little water and fold the plain half of the dough over, as when making a Cornish pasty. Seal the edges by crimping them together with your fingers.

4 Place the calzoni on the greased baking sheets. Brush the tops lightly with olive oil and bake in the preheated oven for 15–20 minutes or until each calzone is puffed up and golden. Serve hot or cold.

COOK'S TIP
Calzoni are the perfect food for picnics and you can vary the fillings to suit the guests. For cocktail parties, you can make miniature versions, known as calzonetti.

Pizza Marinara

INGREDIENTS

60ml/4 tbsp olive oil
675g/1½lb plum tomatoes, peeled, seeded and chopped
30cm/12in pizza base
4 garlic cloves, cut into slivers
15ml/1 tbsp chopped fresh oregano
salt and ground black pepper

SERVES 2–4

1 Preheat the oven to 220°C/425°F/Gas 7. Heat 30ml/2 tbsp of the oil in a saucepan. Add the chopped tomatoes and cook, stirring frequently, for about 5 minutes until softened.

2 Tip the tomatoes into a sieve placed over a bowl. Leave them to drain for about 5 minutes, then transfer them to a food processor or blender. Purée until smooth.

3 Brush the pizza base with half of the remaining oil. Spoon the tomatoes over the base to within 1cm/½ in of the rim, then sprinkle with the garlic and chopped fresh oregano.

4 Then drizzle the remaining oil over the pizza and season with plenty of salt and ground black pepper. Bake the pizza in the preheated oven for 15–20 minutes or until the crust is crisp and golden. Serve at once.

COOK'S TIP
If you are in a hurry, you can substitute two 400g/14oz cans of chopped tomatoes with herbs for the fresh tomatoes. Drain them very well for at least 10 minutes, mash them lightly in the sieve and then spread them directly on to the pizza base. There is no need to purée them first.

82

Meat & Chicken Pizzas

Prosciutto, Mushroom & Artichoke Pizza

INGREDIENTS

1 bunch spring onions
60ml/4 tbsp olive oil
225g/8oz/2 cups mushrooms, sliced
2 garlic cloves, crushed
30cm/12in pizza base
8 slices of prosciutto
4 drained bottled artichoke hearts in oil, sliced
60ml/4 tbsp grated Parmesan cheese
salt and ground black pepper
fresh thyme sprigs, to garnish

SERVES 2–4

1 Preheat the oven to 220°C/425°F/Gas 7. Trim the spring onions, then chop all the white and a little of the green stems finely.

2 Heat 30ml/2 tbsp of the oil in a frying pan. Add the spring onions, mushrooms and garlic and fry over a moderately high heat for about 5 minutes until the  mushrooms are golden and all the juices have evaporated. Add salt and pepper and leave to cool.

3 Brush the pizza base with half the remaining oil. Arrange the prosciutto and artichoke hearts to within 1cm/½in of the rim. Spoon the mushroom  mixture over the top. Sprinkle over the Parmesan, then drizzle with the remaining oil. Bake for 15–20 minutes or until the crust is crisp and golden. Garnish with thyme sprigs and serve at once.

Chicken, Shiitake Mushroom & Coriander Pizza

INGREDIENTS

45ml/3 tbsp olive oil
*350g/12oz skinless, boneless chicken breasts,
cut into thin strips*
1 bunch spring onions, sliced
1 fresh red chilli, seeded and chopped
1 red pepper, seeded and cut into thin strips
*75g/3oz fresh shiitake mushrooms, trimmed
and sliced*
45–60ml/3–4 tbsp chopped fresh coriander
30cm/12in pizza base
15ml/1 tbsp Chilli Oil
*150g/5oz/scant 1 cup grated mozzarella
cheese*
salt and ground black pepper

SERVES 2–4

1 Preheat the oven to 220°C/425°F/Gas 7. Heat 30ml/2 tbsp of the olive oil in a wok or large frying pan. Add the chicken, spring onions, chilli, pepper and mushrooms. Stir-fry over a high heat for 2–3 minutes until the chicken is firm but still slightly pink inside. Add salt and pepper to taste.

2 Pour off any excess oil from the wok or frying pan. Allow the mixture to cool for 5 minutes, then stir in the chopped fresh coriander.

3 Brush the pizza base with the chilli oil. Spoon over the chicken and mushroom mixture to within 1cm/½in of the rim. Drizzle the remaining oil over the pizza.

4 Sprinkle the mozzarella over the pizza. Bake for 15–20 minutes or until the crust is crisp and golden. Serve at once.

Chorizo & Sweetcorn Pizza

INGREDIENTS

30cm/12in pizza base
15ml/1 tbsp Garlic Oil
1 quantity Tomato Sauce
175g/6oz chorizo sausages
50g/2oz/1/3 cup grated mozzarella cheese
30ml/2 tbsp grated Parmesan cheese
*175g/6oz/1 cup drained canned sweetcorn
kernels*
30ml/2 tbsp chopped fresh flat-leaf parsley

SERVES 2–4

3 Then remove the pizza from the oven and sprinkle the sweetcorn and flat-leaf parsley over the top, followed by the mozzarella mixture. Return the pizza

to the oven and bake for 5–10 minutes more until the crust is crisp and golden. Serve at once.

1 Preheat the oven to 220°C/425°F/Gas 7. Brush the pizza base with garlic oil and spread over the tomato sauce to within 1cm/1/2in of the rim.

2 Skin the chorizo sausages, cut them into chunks and scatter them over the pizza base. Bake for 10 minutes. Meanwhile, mix together the mozzarella and Parmesan cheeses in a mixing bowl.

Pancetta, Leek & Smoked Mozzarella Pizzas

INGREDIENTS

2 leeks
30ml/2 tbsp grated Parmesan cheese
1 quantity Basic Pizza Dough
30ml/2 tbsp olive oil
8–12 slices of pancetta
150g/5oz/scant 1 cup grated smoked mozzarella cheese
ground black pepper

SERVES 4

2 Dust the work surface with the Parmesan, then knead it into the dough. Divide the dough into four pieces and roll each one out to a 13cm/5in round.

Place well apart on the greased baking sheets, then push up the edge of the dough on each round to make a rim.

3 Brush half the oil over the pizza bases. Arrange the pancetta and leeks on top, then sprinkle over the grated smoked mozzarella cheese. Drizzle over the

remaining oil and season with plenty of black pepper. Bake for 15–20 minutes or until the crust on each pizza is crisp and golden. Serve at once.

1 Preheat the oven to 220°C/425°F/ Gas 7. Lightly grease two large baking sheets. Trim the leeks and slice them thinly. Wash them in a colander under cold running water and drain well.

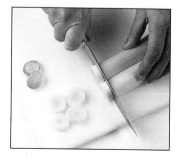

Caramelized Onion, Salami & Olive Pizza

INGREDIENTS

60ml/4 tbsp olive oil
675g/1½lb red onions, thinly sliced
12 stoned black olives, finely chopped
5ml/1 tsp dried herbes de Provence
1 quantity Basic Pizza Dough
6–8 slices of Italian salami, quartered
30–45ml/2–3 tbsp grated Parmesan cheese
ground black pepper

SERVES 4

1 Preheat the oven to 220°C/425°F/ Gas 7. Heat 30ml/2 tbsp of the oil in a frying pan. Add the onions, stir once, then cover with foil or a lid. Cook

over a gentle heat for about 20 minutes, stirring occasionally, until the onions are soft and very lightly coloured. Leave to cool.

2 On a lightly floured surface, knead the olives and herbs into the dough until evenly distributed. Roll out the dough and line a 30 x 18cm/12 x 7in Swiss roll tin. Push up the dough at the edges to make a thin rim all around. Brush the pizza base with half the remaining oil.

3 Spoon half of the caramelized onions over the pizza base. Cover them with the salami, then top with the remaining onions. Grind over plenty of

black pepper and drizzle over the remaining oil.

4 Bake for 15–20 minutes or until the crust is crisp and golden. Remove from the oven and sprinkle the Parmesan over the pizza. Serve at once.

COOK'S TIP

If you are not keen on olives, use slivers of sun-dried tomatoes instead. Buy the type that are bottled in oil, drain them well, and use some of the oil for brushing the dough.

90

Ham & Pineapple French Bread Pizzas

INGREDIENTS

4 small baguettes
1 quantity Tomato Sauce
75g/3oz sliced cooked ham
4 drained canned pineapple rings, chopped
½ small green pepper, seeded and cut into thin strips
75g/3oz/¾ cup grated mature Cheddar cheese
salt and ground black pepper

SERVES 4

1 Preheat the oven to 200°C/400°F/Gas 6. Also preheat the grill. Cut the baguettes in half lengthways. Toast the cut sides under the grill until crisp and golden.

2 Then spread the tomato sauce over the toasted baguettes. Cut the ham into strips and arrange on top, with the pineapple chunks and green pepper strips. Season with plenty of salt and pepper.

3 Sprinkle the grated Cheddar cheese evenly over the topped baguettes. Place on a lightly greased baking sheet and bake for 15–20 minutes until crisp and golden.

COOK'S TIP
You can save energy by grilling the French bread pizzas instead of baking them, if you prefer.

Smoked Chicken, Tomato & Pepper Pizzettes

INGREDIENTS

1 quantity Basic Pizza Dough
45ml/3 tbsp olive oil
60ml/4 tbsp sun-dried tomato paste
2 yellow peppers, seeded and cut into thin strips
175g/6oz sliced smoked chicken or turkey, chopped
150g/5oz/scant 1 cup diced mozzarella cheese
30ml/2 tbsp shredded fresh basil
salt and ground black pepper

SERVES 4

1 Preheat the oven to 220°C/425°F/ Gas 7. Lightly grease two large baking sheets. Divide the dough into four pieces and roll each one out on a lightly floured surface to a 13cm/5in round. Place well apart on the greased baking sheets, then push up the edge of the dough on each round to make a thin rim. Brush with 15ml/1 tbsp of the oil.

2 Spread the pizza bases generously with the sun-dried tomato paste. Heat half the remaining oil in a frying pan and stir-fry the pepper strips for about 4 minutes. Arrange them on the pizza bases, with the smoked chicken or turkey.

3 Scatter over the mozzarella and basil. Season with plenty of salt and black pepper, then drizzle over the remaining oil. Bake for 15–20 minutes or until the crust on each pizzette is crisp and golden. Serve at once.

93

Pepperoni Pan Pizza

INGREDIENTS

115g/4oz/1 cup self-raising white flour
115g/4oz/1 cup self-raising wholemeal flour
pinch of salt
15ml/1 tbsp chopped fresh mixed herbs
50g/2oz/¼ cup butter, diced
about 150ml/¼ pint/⅔ cup milk
TOPPING
30ml/2 tbsp tomato purée
400g/14oz can chopped tomatoes, well drained
50g/2oz/½ cup button mushrooms, thinly sliced
75g/3oz sliced pepperoni
6 stoned black olives, chopped
115g/4oz/1 cup grated mature Cheddar cheese
15ml/1 tbsp shredded fresh basil, to garnish

SERVES 2–4

2 Cook the dough in the pan over a low heat for about 5 minutes, until the base is golden. Invert a baking sheet over the pan, then carefully flip the sheet and pan over to invert the pizza.

3 Slide the pizza base back into the pan, cooked side up. Spread over the tomato purée, then spoon the tomatoes on top. Scatter over the remaining ingredients and cook for 5 minutes more, until the underside of the pizza is golden. Preheat the grill.

4 Slide the pan under the grill and cook for about 5 minutes, until the cheese has melted and the topping is bubbling. Sprinkle the shredded fresh basil over the pizza and serve at once.

1 Grease a 22cm/8½in frying pan which can be used under the grill. Mix the flours, salt and herbs in a large bowl. Rub in the butter until the mixture resembles fine breadcrumbs. Mix in the milk very quickly to make a soft dough, then knead gently on a lightly floured surface until smooth. Roll out to fit the frying pan.

COOK'S TIP
If you prefer, place the scone dough round on a baking sheet, add the topping and bake it in an oven preheated to 220°C/425°F/ Gas 7 for 20–25 minutes.

Fish & Seafood Pizzas

Prawn & Basil Pizzettes

INGREDIENTS

1 quantity Basic Pizza Dough
30ml/2 tbsp Chilli Oil
75g/3oz/½ cup grated mozzarella cheese
1 garlic clove, chopped
½ small red onion, thinly sliced
4–6 pieces of drained sun-dried tomatoes in oil, thinly sliced
115g/4oz cooked prawns, peeled and deveined
60ml/4 tbsp shredded fresh basil
salt and ground black pepper

SERVES 4

1 Preheat the oven to 220°C/425°F/ Gas 7. Grease two large baking sheets. Pat out the dough to a thick round, then cut the round into eight equal-size wedges.

2 Roll out each wedge of dough on a lightly floured surface to a small oval, about 5mm/¼in thick. Place well apart on the greased baking sheets. Prick the dough all over with a fork.

3 Brush the pizza bases with 15ml/1 tbsp of the chilli oil. Top with the grated mozzarella cheese, leaving a clear 1cm/½in border all the way around the edge.

4 Divide the garlic, onion, sun-dried tomatoes, prawns and half the basil among the pizza bases. Add salt and pepper and drizzle the remaining chilli oil over the top. Bake for 8–10 minutes or until the crust on each pizzette is crisp and golden. Serve at once, sprinkled with the remaining basil.

Seafood Pizza

INGREDIENTS

*450g/1lb peeled plum tomatoes or 2
400g/14oz cans chopped tomatoes, drained
175g/6oz small squid
225g/8oz fresh mussels
30cm/12in pizza base
175g/6oz raw or cooked prawns, peeled and
deveined
2 garlic cloves, finely chopped
45ml/3 tbsp chopped fresh parsley
30ml/2 tbsp olive oil
salt and ground black pepper*

SERVES 4

1 Preheat the oven to 220°C/425°F/Gas 7. Strain the tomatoes through the medium holes of a food mill or sieve placed over a bowl, scraping in all the pulp. If you use canned tomatoes, drain them for at least 10 minutes before straining, or the topping will be too sloppy.

2 Prepare the squid by holding the body in one hand and gently pulling away the head and tentacles. Discard the head; chop the tentacles roughly. Keeping the body sac whole, remove the transparent "quill" from inside, then peel off the brown skin on the outside. Rinse the sac, rub with salt and rinse again. Drain, then slice into 5mm/¼ in rings.

3 Carefully scrub the mussels, pulling off the beards and discarding any which are open. Place the mussels in a saucepan with a close-fitting lid. Add about 45ml/ 3 tbsp water. Close the pan tightly and shake over the heat until the mussels open. Transfer them to a dish, discarding any that remain closed.

4 Spread some of the puréed tomatoes on the pizza base to within 1cm/½in of the rim. Dot the prawns and the prepared squid evenly over the tomatoes. Sprinkle with the garlic and parsley. Season with plenty of salt and pepper, then drizzle with the olive oil.

5 Bake for 8 minutes, then remove from the oven and add the mussels on the half shell. Bake for 7–10 minutes more or until the crust is crisp and golden. Serve at once.

Crab & Parmesan Calzonetti

INGREDIENTS

1 quantity Basic Pizza Dough
115g/4oz mixed prepared crab meat, thawed
if frozen
15ml/1 tbsp double cream
30ml/2 tbsp grated Parmesan cheese
30ml/2 tbsp chopped fresh parsley
1 garlic clove, crushed
salt and ground black pepper
fresh parsley sprigs, to garnish

MAKES 10–12

100

1 Preheat the oven to 220°C/425°F/Gas 7. Grease two large baking sheets. Roll out the dough on a lightly floured surface to a thickness of 3mm/⅛in. Using a 7.5cm/3in plain round cutter, stamp out 10–12 rounds and set them aside.

2 Make the filling by mixing the crab meat, cream, Parmesan, chopped fresh parsley and crushed garlic in a bowl. Season with salt and ground pepper to taste.

3 Spoon a little of the filling on to one half of each circle. Dampen the edges with water and fold over to enclose the filling. Seal the edges with a fork.

Place the calzonetti well apart on the greased baking sheets and bake for 10–15 minutes, until golden. Garnish with fresh parsley sprigs and serve.

VARIATION
Use prawns instead of crab meat if you prefer.

Mussel & Leek Pizzettes

INGREDIENTS

450g/1lb fresh mussels
120ml/4fl oz/½ cup dry white wine
1 quantity Basic Pizza Dough
15ml/1 tbsp olive oil
50g/2oz/½ cup grated Gruyère cheese
50g/2oz/½ cup grated mozzarella cheese
2 small leeks, sliced
salt and ground black pepper

SERVES 4

1 Preheat the oven to 220°C/425°F/Gas 7. Grease two large baking sheets. Carefully scrub the mussels, pull off the beards and discard any which are open. Place the mussels in a pan.

2 Add the dry white wine, close the pan lid tightly and shake over the heat until the mussels open. Transfer the mussels to a dish, discarding any that remain closed, then remove them from their shells and leave them to cool.

3 Divide the dough into four pieces and roll each one out on a lightly floured surface to a 13cm/5in round. Place well apart on the greased baking sheets, then push up the edge of the dough on each round to make a thin rim. Brush the bases with the oil and sprinkle with half the mixed cheeses.

4 Scatter the leeks over the cheese. Bake for 10 minutes, then arrange the mussels on top of the pizzettes. Season with salt and pepper. Sprinkle with the remaining mixed cheeses and bake for 5–10 minutes more, until the crust on each pizzette is crisp and golden. Serve at once.

Anchovy, Pepper & Tomato Pizza

INGREDIENTS

6 plum tomatoes
45ml/3 tbsp olive oil
5ml/1 tsp salt
1 large red pepper
1 large yellow pepper
30cm/12in pizza base
2 garlic cloves, chopped
50g/2oz can anchovy fillets, drained
ground black pepper
fresh basil leaves, to garnish

SERVES 2–4

1 Cut the tomatoes in half lengthways and scoop out the seeds. Chop the flesh roughly and place it in a bowl. Add 15ml/1 tbsp of the oil and the salt. Mix well, then cover and leave to marinate for 30 minutes.

2 Meanwhile, preheat the oven to 220°C/425°F/ Gas 7, and the grill to high. Slice the peppers in half lengthways and remove the core and seeds. Arrange the pepper halves, skin side up, on a baking sheet. Grill until the skins are evenly charred.

3 Place the peppers in a heatproof bowl. Cover with several layers of kitchen paper and leave for 10–15 minutes. Peel off the pepper skins and cut the flesh into thin strips.

4 Brush the pizza base with half the remaining oil. Drain the marinated tomatoes and scatter them over the base to within 1cm/½in of the pizza rim. Arrange the peppers and garlic evenly over the pizza base.

5 Snip up the anchovy fillets into small pieces and sprinkle them over the pizza base. Season with ground black pepper. Drizzle over the remaining oil and bake for 15–20 minutes or until the crust is crisp and golden. Serve at once, garnished with the whole fresh basil leaves.

Tuna, Anchovy & Caper Scone Pizza

INGREDIENTS

115g/4oz/1 cup self-raising white flour
115g/4oz/1 cup self-raising wholemeal flour
· pinch of salt
50g/2oz/¼ cup butter, diced
about 150ml/¼ pint/⅔ cup milk
TOPPING
30ml/2 tbsp olive oil
1 quantity Tomato Sauce
1 small red onion, cut in thin wedges
200g/7oz can tuna, drained and flaked
15ml/1 tbsp drained capers
12 stoned black olives
45ml/3 tbsp grated Parmesan cheese
50g/2oz can anchovy fillets, drained and
halved lengthways
ground black pepper

SERVES 2–4

1 Preheat the oven to 220°C/425°F/Gas 7. Mix the flours and salt in a large bowl. Rub in the butter until the mixture resembles fine breadcrumbs. Mix in the milk very quickly to make a soft dough, then knead gently on a lightly floured surface and roll out to a 25cm/10in round.

2 Brush the scone dough base with 15ml/1 tbsp of the oil. Spread the tomato sauce to within 1cm/½in of the rim, then arrange the onion wedges and flaked tuna on top. Dot with the capers and olives, then sprinkle with the Parmesan.

3 Make a lattice with the anchovy fillets on top of the pizza. Drizzle over the remaining oil and add a generous grinding of black pepper. Bake in the preheated oven for 15–20 minutes or until the scone crust is crisp and golden. Serve at once.

Salmon & Avocado Pizza

INGREDIENTS

150g/5oz salmon fillet
120ml/4fl oz/½ cup white wine
30cm/12in pizza base
15ml/1 tbsp olive oil
400g/14oz can chopped tomatoes, well drained
115g/4oz/⅔ cup grated mozzarella cheese
1 small avocado
10ml/2 tsp lemon juice
30ml/2 tbsp crème fraîche
75g/3oz smoked salmon, cut into strips
15ml/1 tbsp drained capers
30ml/2 tbsp snipped fresh chives, to garnish
ground black pepper

SERVES 2–4

105

1 Preheat the oven to 220°C/425°F/ Gas 7. Place the salmon fillet in a frying pan, pour over the wine and season with black pepper. Bring slowly to the boil,

remove the pan from the heat, cover and let the fish finish cooking in the cooling liquid. Skin the salmon and flake it finely, removing any bones.

2 Brush the pizza base with the oil and spread the drained tomatoes over the base to within 1cm/½in of the rim. Sprinkle over half the grated mozzarella. Bake for 10 minutes.

3 Meanwhile, cut the avocado in half. Lift out the stone, remove the peel and slice the flesh into small cubes. Toss with the lemon juice in a bowl.

4 Remove the pizza from the oven, dot with crème fraîche and arrange the fresh and smoked salmon on top. Add the drained avocado cubes, capers and remaining mozzarella, with black pepper. Bake for 5–10 minutes more or until the crust is crisp and golden. Sprinkle with the chives and serve at once.

Vegetarian Pizzas

Fresh Vegetable Pizza

INGREDIENTS

450g/1lb peeled plum tomatoes or 2
400g/14oz cans chopped tomatoes, drained
3 small courgettes, trimmed
2 broccoli spears, broken into small florets
225g/8oz fresh asparagus spears, trimmed and
cut into short lengths
45ml/3 tbsp olive oil
50g/2oz/½ cup shelled peas, fresh or
thawed frozen
4 spring onions, sliced
30cm/12in pizza base
75g/3oz/½ cup diced mozzarella cheese
10 fresh basil leaves, torn into pieces
2 garlic cloves, finely chopped
salt and ground black pepper

SERVES 2–4

I Preheat the oven to 220°C/425°F/Gas 7. Strain the tomatoes through the medium holes of a food mill or sieve placed over a bowl, scraping in all the pulp. If you use canned tomatoes, drain them for at least 10 minutes before straining, or the topping will be too sloppy.

2 Slice the courgettes lengthways, keeping them intact at one end. Bring a saucepan of lightly salted water to the boil, add the broccoli, asparagus and courgettes and blanch for 4–5 minutes. Drain well.

3 Heat 30ml/2 tbsp of the olive oil in a saucepan. Stir-fry the peas and spring onions for 5 minutes. Spread the puréed tomatoes over the pizza base to within 1cm/½in of the rim. Arrange the blanched and stir-fried vegetables on top, fanning out the courgettes.

4 Sprinkle with the mozzarella, basil, garlic, salt and pepper. Drizzle the remaining oil over the top and bake for 15–20 minutes or until the crust is crisp and golden. Serve at once.

Roasted Vegetable & Goat's Cheese Pizza

INGREDIENTS

1 aubergine, cut into thick chunks
2 small courgettes, sliced lengthways
1 red pepper, quartered and seeded
1 yellow pepper, quartered and seeded
1 small red onion, cut into wedges
90ml/6 tbsp Garlic Oil
1 goat's cheese, about 115g/4oz
30cm/12in pizza base
400g/14oz can chopped tomatoes, well drained
15ml/1 tbsp chopped fresh thyme
ground black pepper
green olive tapenade, to serve

SERVES 2–4

1 Preheat the oven to 220°C/425°F/ Gas 7. Place the aubergine, courgette slices, peppers and onion in a large roasting tin. (The peppers should be skin-side up.) Brush with 60ml/4 tbsp of the garlic oil. Roast for 30 minutes until lightly charred, turning the peppers over halfway through cooking.

2 Meanwhile, without removing the rind, cut the goat's cheese into cubes. Remove the roasting tin from the oven. Transfer the peppers to a bowl, cover with several layers of kitchen paper and leave for 10–15 minutes.

3 Peel the skins from the peppers and cut the flesh into thick strips. Brush the pizza base with half the remaining garlic oil and spread the drained chopped

tomatoes over the base to within 1cm/½ in of the rim. Arrange the roasted vegetables and goat's cheese on top.

4 Then scatter the chopped thyme over the pizza and drizzle with the remaining garlic oil. Season with a generous grinding of black pepper. Bake in the preheated oven for 15–20 minutes or until the crust

is crisp and golden. Spoon over the green olive tapenade and serve at once.

Fresh Herb & Garlic Pizza

INGREDIENTS

*115g/4oz/2 cups fresh mixed herbs, such as
parsley, basil and oregano
3 garlic cloves, crushed
120ml/4fl oz/½ cup double cream
30cm/12in pizza base
15ml/1 tbsp Garlic Oil
115g/4oz/1 cup grated Pecorino cheese
salt and ground black pepper*

SERVES 4

1 Preheat the oven to 220°C/425°F/ Gas 7. Place the mixed herbs on a board and chop with a mezzaluna. Alternatively, you can pulse the herbs in a food processor, but be careful not to allow them to form a paste.

2 Tip the herbs into a mixing bowl and add the garlic and cream. Season with plenty of salt and pepper, then mix well.

3 Brush the pizza base with the garlic oil, then spread the herb mixture over the top to within 1cm/½ in of the rim. Sprinkle over the Pecorino.

4 Bake the pizza in the oven for 15–20 minutes or until the crust is crisp and golden. Serve at once.

110

COOK'S TIP
This pizza makes a wonderfully flavoursome cocktail snack. Cut the pizza into eight thin wedges before serving.

Wild Mushroom Pizzettes

INGREDIENTS

45ml/3 tbsp olive oil
350g/12oz/3 cups fresh wild mushrooms,
washed and sliced
2 shallots, chopped
2 garlic cloves, crushed
30ml/2 tbsp chopped fresh mixed thyme and
flat-leaf parsley
1 quantity Basic Pizza Dough
50g/2oz/½ cup grated Gruyère cheese
30ml/2 tbsp grated Parmesan cheese
salt and ground black pepper

SERVES 4

2 Divide the dough into four pieces and roll each one out on a lightly floured surface to a 13cm/5in round. Place on the greased baking sheets, then push up the edge of the dough on each round to make a thin rim.

3 Brush the pizzette bases with the remaining oil and top with the mushroom mixture. Mix the Gruyère and Parmesan cheeses and sprinkle them over. Bake for 15–20 minutes or until the crust on each pizzette is crisp and golden. Sprinkle with the remaining herbs and serve at once.

111

I Preheat the oven to 220°C/425°F/ Gas 7. Grease two large baking sheets. Heat 30ml/2 tbsp of the oil in a frying pan. Add the mushrooms, shallots and garlic and

cook over a moderately high heat for about 5 minutes, until the mushrooms are golden and most of the juices have evaporated. Stir in half the herbs, with salt and pepper to taste. Leave to cool.

Tomato, Pesto & Black Olive Pizzettes

INGREDIENTS

2 plum tomatoes
1 garlic clove, crushed
60ml/4 tbsp olive oil
1 quantity Basic Pizza Dough
30ml/2 tbsp red pesto
150g/5oz mozzarella cheese, thinly sliced
4 stoned black olives, chopped
15ml/1 tbsp chopped fresh oregano
salt and ground black pepper
fresh oregano leaves, to garnish

SERVES 4

1 Cut the tomatoes in half, then slice them thinly. Place the tomatoes and the crushed garlic in a shallow bowl, drizzle over 30ml/2 tbsp of the oil and sprinkle with salt and pepper. Leave to marinate for 15 minutes.

2 Preheat the oven to 220°C/425°F/Gas 7. Grease two large baking sheets. Divide the dough into four pieces and roll each one out on a lightly floured surface to a 13cm/5in round. Place the bases well apart on the greased baking sheets, then push up the edge of the dough on each base to make a thin rim.

3 Then brush the pizzette bases with half the remaining oil and spread over the red pesto. Drain the tomatoes and arrange a fan of alternate slices of

tomatoes and mozzarella on each base.

4 Dot the pizzettes with the olives and sprinkle with the chopped oregano. Drizzle with the remaining oil and bake for 15–20 minutes or until the crust on each pizzette is crisp and golden. Garnish with the whole fresh oregano leaves and serve at once.

Red Onion & Gorgonzola Pizza Bites

INGREDIENTS

1 quantity Basic Pizza Dough
30ml/2 tbsp Garlic Oil
2 small red onions, halved, then sliced into
thin wedges
150g/5oz Gorgonzola piccante
2 garlic cloves, cut into thin slivers
10ml/2 tsp chopped fresh sage
ground black pepper

SERVES 4

1 Preheat the oven to 220°C/425°F/ Gas 7. Lightly grease two baking sheets. Divide the pizza dough into eight pieces and roll out each piece to a small oval

about 5mm/¼in thick. Place the pizza bases well apart on the greased baking sheets and prick them all over with a fork. Brush the bases with 15ml/1 tbsp of the garlic oil.

2 Then scatter the onion wedges over the bases. Remove the rind from the Gorgonzola and cut the cheese into small cubes. Scatter the Gorgonzola cubes over the onion wedges.

3 Sprinkle the garlic slivers over the Gorgonzola cubes, with the chopped fresh sage. Drizzle over the remaining oil. Add a generous grinding of black pepper and bake for 15–20 minutes or until the crust is crisp and golden. Serve at once.

Onion & Three Cheese Pizza

INGREDIENTS

45ml/3 tbsp olive oil
3 onions, sliced
30cm/12in pizza base
4 small tomatoes, peeled, seeded and cut into thin wedges
30ml/2 tbsp shredded fresh basil
115g/4oz Dolcelatte cheese
150g/5oz mozzarella cheese
115g/4oz Red Leicester cheese
ground black pepper
fresh basil leaves, to garnish

SERVES 4

2 Brush the pizza base with the remaining oil. Spoon over the onions and tomatoes, then scatter the shredded basil over the top.

3 Slice the cheeses thinly and arrange the slices over the tomatoes and the onions. Add a generous grinding of black pepper. Bake for 15–20 minutes or until the crust is crisp and golden. Sprinkle with fresh basil leaves to garnish and serve at once.

1 Preheat the oven to 220°C/425°F/ Gas 7. Heat 30ml/2 tbsp of the oil in a frying pan. Add the onions and fry over a gentle heat for about 10 min-

utes, stirring occasionally, until the onions are soft. Leave to cool.

114

Feta, Roasted Garlic & Oregano Pizzettes

INGREDIENTS

1 garlic bulb
45ml/3 tbsp olive oil
1 red pepper, quartered and seeded
1 yellow pepper, quartered and seeded
1 quantity Basic Pizza Dough
2 plum tomatoes, peeled, seeded and chopped
175g/6oz/1 cup feta cheese, crumbled
ground black pepper
15–30ml/1–2 tbsp shredded fresh oregano, to garnish

SERVES 4

1 Preheat the oven to 220°C/425°F/Gas 7 and also the grill to high. Grease two large baking sheets. Break the garlic into cloves, discarding the papery outer layers, but leaving the skin on the cloves. Put them in a bowl and toss with 15ml/1 tbsp of the oil.

2 Grill the peppers, skin-side up, until the skins are evenly charred. Place them in a heatproof bowl. Cover with several layers of kitchen paper and leave for 10–15 minutes. Peel off the pepper skins and cut the flesh into thin strips.

3 Divide the dough into four pieces and roll each one out on a lightly floured surface to a 13cm/5in round. Place the rounds well apart on the greased baking sheets, then push up the edge of the dough on each round to make a thin rim.

4 Brush over half the remaining oil and scatter over the chopped tomatoes. Top with the peppers, feta and garlic cloves. Drizzle over the remaining oil and season with black pepper. Bake for 15–20 minutes or until the crust on each pizzette is crisp and golden. Garnish with the oregano and serve at once.

Party Pizzas

Smoked Salmon Pizzettes

INGREDIENTS

15ml/1 tbsp finely snipped fresh chives
1 quantity Basic Pizza Dough
15ml/1 tbsp olive oil
75–115g/3–4oz smoked salmon,
cut into strips
60ml/4 tbsp crème fraîche
30ml/2 tbsp black lumpfish roe
halved fresh chives, to garnish

MAKES 10–12

1 Preheat the oven to 200°C/400°F/ Gas 6. Lightly grease two large baking sheets. On a lightly floured surface, knead the finely snipped chives into the pizza dough until they are evenly distributed. Roll out the dough to a thickness of about 3mm/⅛in. Using a 7.5cm/3in plain round cutter, stamp out 10–12 rounds.

2 Place the pizzette bases well apart on the greased baking sheets. Prick them all over with a fork, then brush with the olive oil. Bake for 10–12 minutes, until each base is crisp and golden.

3 Arrange the strips of smoked salmon on top of the pizzettes, folding them to avoid overlapping the edges. Place a spoonful of crème fraîche in the centre of each pizzette and add a tiny amount of lumpfish roe in the centre. Garnish with the fresh chives and serve at once.

117

Spinach & Ricotta Panzerotti

INGREDIENTS

115g/4oz frozen chopped spinach, thawed,
drained and squeezed dry
50g/2oz/¼ cup ricotta cheese
50g/2oz/⅓ cup grated Parmesan cheese
generous pinch of grated nutmeg
double quantity Basic Pizza Dough
1 egg white, lightly beaten
vegetable oil, for deep-frying
salt and ground black pepper

MAKES 20–24

1 Mix the spinach, ricotta, Parmesan and nutmeg in a bowl. Stir in salt and pepper to taste, then beat until smooth.

2 Roll out the dough on a lightly floured surface to a thickness of about 3mm/⅛in. Using a 7.5cm/ 3in plain cutter, stamp out 20–24 rounds. Spread

about a teaspoon of spinach mixture on one half of each circle, leaving the outer rim clear.

3 Brush the edges of the dough with a little egg white, fold the uncovered half of each round of dough over the filling and press the edges firmly together to seal.

4 Heat the oil for deep-frying in a large saucepan or deep-fryer. Add the panzerotti, a few at a time, and deep-fry for about 3 minutes, until they are crisp and golden. Remove them from the pan with a slotted spoon and drain on kitchen paper. Keep the cooked panzerotti hot while deep-frying the subsequent batches, but do not leave them for too long before serving; they are at their best when freshly fried.

VARIATION

Chop five drained artichoke hearts finely and use them instead of the spinach for an unusual and very tasty filling.

Quick Party Pizza Bites

INGREDIENTS

115g/4oz/1 cup self-raising white flour
115g/4oz/1 cup self-raising wholemeal flour
pinch of salt
50g/2oz/¼ cup butter, diced
10 fresh basil leaves, plus extra to garnish
about 150ml/¼ pint/⅔ cup milk
TOPPING
115g/4oz/⅔ cup drained sun-dried tomatoes
in oil, chopped, plus 30ml/2 tbsp
oil from jar
1 quantity Tomato Sauce
10 stoned black olives, chopped
15ml/1 tbsp shredded fresh basil
50g/2oz/½ cup grated mozzarella cheese
30ml/2 tbsp grated Parmesan cheese

MAKES 24

1 Preheat the oven to 220°C/425°F/Gas 7. Mix the flours and salt in a large bowl. Rub in the butter until the mixture resembles fine breadcrumbs. Tear the basil leaves roughly, then add them to the mixture. Mix in the milk quickly to make a soft dough.

2 Knead the dough gently on a lightly floured surface until smooth. Roll out and line a 30 x 18cm/12 x 7in Swiss roll tin. Push up the edges to make a thin rim.

3 Brush the base with 15ml/1 tbsp of the tomato oil, then spread over the tomato sauce. Scatter the sun-dried tomatoes and olives over the top, with the shredded basil.

4 Mix the cheeses in a bowl, then sprinkle them over the pizza base. Drizzle over the remaining tomato oil. Bake for about 20 minutes in the preheated oven. Cut into 24 bite-size pieces, garnish with extra shredded basil leaves and serve at once.

Mini Pizzas with Mozzarella, Anchovy & Pesto

INGREDIENTS

*2 ready-to-cook pizza bases, about 20cm/8in
in diameter
60ml/4 tbsp olive oil
30ml/2 tbsp red pesto
12 stoned black olives
75g/3oz/½ cup diced mozzarella cheese
50g/2oz/⅓ cup drained sun-dried tomatoes
in oil, chopped
30–45ml/2–3 tbsp drained capers
50g/2oz can anchovy fillets, drained and
roughly chopped
30ml/2 tbsp grated Parmesan cheese
fresh parsley sprigs, to garnish*

MAKES 24

121

1 Preheat the oven to 220°C/425°F/Gas 7. Grease two large baking sheets. Using a 5cm/2in plain round cutter, stamp out 24 rounds from the pizza bases and arrange them on the baking sheets. Brush the bases with 30ml/2 tbsp of the oil, then spread with the pesto.

2 Cut the olives lengthways into quarters. Arrange on top of the pizza bases, with the mozzarella, sun-dried tomatoes, capers and anchovies.

3 Sprinkle over the Parmesan, then drizzle with the remaining oil. Bake for 8–10 minutes or until the crust on each mini pizza is crisp and golden. Garnish with fresh parsley sprigs and serve at once.

COOK'S TIP
If you are in a hurry, just add the topping to the whole pizza bases. When cooked, cut them into slender wedges for serving.

Tomato & Basil Tart

INGREDIENTS

175g/6oz/1½ cups plain flour
2.5ml/½ tsp salt
115g/4oz/½ cup butter or margarine, chilled
45–75ml/3–5 tbsp cold water
TOPPING
30ml/2 tbsp extra-virgin olive oil
175g/6oz mozzarella cheese, very thinly sliced
12 fresh basil leaves
4–5 tomatoes, sliced
60ml/4 tbsp grated Parmesan cheese
salt and ground black pepper

SERVES 6–8

1 Mix the flour and salt in a large bowl. Rub in the butter or margarine until the mixture resembles fine breadcrumbs, then add just enough water to bind the dough. Gather the pastry into a ball, flatten it to a disc and wrap in greaseproof paper. Chill for 40 minutes.

2 Preheat the oven to 190°C/375°F/Gas 5. Roll out the pastry on a lightly floured surface and line a 28cm/11in pie tin or pizza pan. Trim the edges evenly. Chill for 10 minutes if you have time.

3 Line the pastry with greaseproof paper and baking beans. Bake blind for 15 minutes, then remove the pastry case from the oven and lift out the paper and beans. Leave the oven on for baking the filled tart.

4 Brush the pastry case with a little of the oil and arrange the mozzarella slices over the surface. Shred half the basil leaves and sprinkle them over the mozzarella, then arrange the tomato slices in concentric circles on top.

5 Dot the surface with the remaining whole basil leaves. Sprinkle with salt and pepper. Spoon the Parmesan over the top and drizzle with the remaining oil. Bake for 35 minutes. Serve hot or at room temperature.

COOK'S TIP

If the melted cheese exudes a lot of liquid during baking, tilt the tin and spoon it off to prevent the pastry from becoming soggy.

122

Farmhouse Pizza

INGREDIENTS

75ml/5 tbsp olive oil
225g/8oz/2 cups button mushrooms, sliced
double quantity Basic Pizza Dough
1 quantity Tomato Sauce
275g/10oz mozzarella cheese, thinly sliced
115g/4oz wafer-thin smoked ham slices
6 drained bottled artichoke hearts in oil, sliced
*50g/2oz can anchovy fillets, drained and
halved lengthways*
10 stoned black olives, halved
30ml/2 tbsp chopped fresh oregano
*45ml/3 tbsp grated Parmesan cheese
ground black pepper*

SERVES 4–6

1 Preheat the oven to 220°C/425°F/ Gas 7. Lightly grease a 30 x 25cm/12 x 10in baking sheet. Heat 30ml/2 tbsp of the oil in a large frying pan. Add  the mushrooms and cook over a moderately high heat for about 5 minutes, until they are golden and most of the juices have evaporated. Leave to cool.

2 Knead the dough gently on a lightly floured surface until smooth. Roll out to fit the greased baking sheet, then push up the dough edges to make a thin rim. Brush with 30ml/2 tbsp of the oil, then spread with the tomato sauce.

3 Arrange the mozzarella slices over the tomato sauce. Scrunch up the smoked ham slices and arrange on top, with the artichoke hearts, mushrooms and  anchovies. Dot with the halved black olives.

4 Sprinkle the chopped fresh oregano and Parmesan cheese over the top of the pizza. Drizzle over the remaining oil and season with plenty of black pepper. Bake for about 25 minutes or until the crust is crisp and golden. Serve at once.

COOK'S TIP
For a special treat, try this pizza with wild mushrooms and prosciutto instead of the button mushrooms and smoked ham.

124

Instant Pizzas

QUICK PIZZA SCONES

Cut fresh scones in half and spread the cut sides with red pesto. Top with a slice of tomato and dried oregano and season to taste. Sprinkle with grated Cheddar cheese and grill until golden and bubbling.

TOASTED ROLLS WITH CHEVRE

Cut bread rolls in half and toast the cut sides. Spread the rolls with home-made tomato sauce, sprinkle with snipped fresh basil and top with slices of chèvre (goat's cheese). Grill until the cheese melts.

CIABATTA WITH MOZZARELLA

Cut a loaf of ciabatta in half and toast the cut sides lightly. Spread with 60ml/4 tbsp red pesto or a mixture of tomato purée and mild red pepper mustard. Slice 2 small onions thickly, brush the slices lightly with olive oil and grill until lightly browned. Top the ciabatta with 225g/8oz sliced mozzarella cheese, arrange the onion slices on top and scatter over some black olives. Grill for about 2 minutes, until the cheese melts and the onion chars.

COOK'S TIP
Although cheeses are best bought in small quantities for immediate consumption, those with a high fat content (above 45 percent) can be frozen. Wrap cheeses carefully and thaw well before using them for cooking or eating.

Index